Headless Brides and Devil Dogs
Exploring Southern Ohio's Haunted Roads and Bridges

By David Alan Scott

Published by Long Moss Publishing,
United States of America

Copyright ©2009, David Alan Scott
All Rights Reserved

No part of this book may be reproduced or utilized in any form or by any means, electronic or mechanical, including photocopying, recording or by any information storage and retrieval system without permission in writing from the author.

Inquiries and/or comments should be addressed through the author's web site at:
http://fallingtimber.net/

Dedication:
To my parents who have been wondering what the heck I have been up to for the past few years. Now you know.

Photo Credits:
All photos were taken by David Alan Scott except those marked with an asterisk (*). Photos marked with an asterisk were used with permission and kindly provided by Don Prout's Cincinnativiews web site, located at -
http://cincinnativiews.net/
Cover photo "Somewhere Near Shandon, Ohio" by David Alan Scott

International Standard Book Number
978-0-578-03124-8

Table of Contents

Introduction.. 4

Dead Man's Curve................................... 7
Buffalo Ridge... 16
Rapid Run Park...................................... 29
Tiny Town/Munchkinland................... 39
Hangman's Hollow................................ 49
The Oxford Motorcycle........................ 54
Pond Run Road...................................... 60
Spooky Hollow Road............................ 65
Lick Road.. 73
The Screaming Bridge of Maud Hughes Road.. 81
The Highway to Heaven....................... 88
The Headless Ghost of Dunlap............. 94
Buell Road.. 98
Princeton Road..................................... 102

Afterword 107
Glossary.. 109

Introduction

I am a paranormal investigator. I can now say that with a straight face. I have always been interested in the strange and the unknown, but it wasn't until my sister moved into a haunted house that I made a real effort to understand just what it is that causes these real and unexplained sights and sounds. The bumps in the night. Things moving for no reason. Disembodied voices and apparitions. What are they? Are they really spirits? Are they beings intersecting our world from some other dimension or alternate universe? What is going on here? My sister's house made a handy testing ground for our experiments and investigations into the barely perceptible world of ghosts and hauntings. We spent many a night taking photos, videos, and audio recordings. Setting up motion sensors and new homemade equipment. Analyzing the data and eliminating anything "natural" which could have been causing the weird phenomena. After spending so many hours at her house, chasing ghosts and successfully gathering evidence, I started searching for other places to investigate. I wanted to expand my horizons and learn even more about the other side.

Not wanting to invade the homes of strangers, I thought it would be a good idea to look for public places. I thought I would find locations that anyone could access, without worrying about other people interfering with the investigation. I especially wanted to avoid the "tourist spots" as I call them – places like abandoned prisons, bed and breakfasts, old asylums, and the other places being overrun with people day after day. In these days of ghost-hunting hysteria, countless paranormal groups seem to be covering the same ground continuously, never really learning anything new. If I saw one more spirit orb photo or a "ghost face" in an old mirror, I was sure I would be sick. I wanted more than just a cheap thrill. I wanted some real evidence and above all, I wanted to investigate new localities.

I began to think of all of the scary places we hear about as we grow up. Every state has them. Tall tales and folklore handed down from person to person. Some of these legends have endured for decades without a shred of evidence to support them. The headless train engineers with their bobbing lanterns, the crybaby bridges, and the phantom hitchhikers along the side of the road. Teenagers everywhere visit these places, just to see if anything scary will happen. They embellish the stories and spread them around. Eventually the stories become part of a region's oral history.

I am fortunate to live in Ohio, a state that is virtually teeming with legends of ghosts and hauntings of all kinds. Since high school, I can remember hearing stories about the creepy things on Buffalo Ridge and the commune of little people who lived back in the woods. I even had some personal experiences such as the time I was driving through Spooky Hollow when my car's headlights suddenly went out for no explainable reason. Greater Cincinnati, and the entire state of Ohio, is filled with these legendary places, full of mystery, just waiting to be explored.

Although I do believe in life after death, I do not believe all of these legends are true. Actually, I think most of them are only stories people have made up in order to entertain themselves and to give people something to wonder about. The purpose of my investigations was to find out the truth behind these legends. Were any of them based on true events? How much, if anything, was true? Were some of the details true and the rest just imaginative tidbits added by people who didn't really know what they were talking about? And were any of these places really haunted? I expected it would take a lot of work to find the answers to these questions. I began my research by investigating a few of the most popular legends and then creating a web site to document my findings. Before long, I began to get e-mail from helpful people who suggested other places for me to investigate. Some wrote to tell me of their own experiences or to give me more information about the places I had visited. Each individual investigation turned into an ongoing project because I was always learning something new or finding reasons to revisit the sites, always gathering more details and taking more photos. As I visited each site, I also tried to gather evidence with the gear I typically use for paranormal investigations – EMF meters, digital audio recorders, infrared cameras, and whatever else I could find to bring along.

Although I try my best to gather evidence of paranormal activity, it has been difficult or nearly impossible to do thorough investigations at some of the locations in this book. When you are trying to do a paranormal investigation in the outdoors, you run into many problems you would never run into if you were investigating the inside of a building. When you are outside, there is usually too much noise to make proper audio recordings, photos may be contaminated by lights from passing cars, and there is all sorts of extraneous electrical interference from street lights, power lines, and other electromagnetic sources.

This book is not a collection of third party stories. I have personally spent over three years investigating every location featured in this book. Some of the places I have visited numerous times. No matter how much I learn about each location, I find that there is more to learn. It's an ongoing process and I feel that I have barely scratched the surface. To research the information in this book, I spent many hours in libraries, I traveled over many roads, and walked along them. I talked to local residents and kept in touch with some of them so I could update information as I compiled it. I tried my best to make sure the information presented here is factual.

Everyone enjoys a good spooky story, but this book is not meant to be a collection of spooky stories. Instead, I have taken each of the legends and investigated them at length in order to find out if they were based on true events. And of course I tried to determine if these places were really haunted. Some of the legends are partially true. Some are crazy unbelievable stories that continue to be handed down in spite of a total lack of evidence, and some are mysterious places and events we still aren't sure about. With each chapter, I try to present the legend along with the source of the story, if any, and then add the information I have gathered through personal research. In some cases, this information blends together, but hopefully I have presented it so that you can easily tell the difference between truth and speculation. As wild as some of the legends are, sometimes the truth behind them is even stranger.

Dead Man's Curve

Most states probably have a piece of road they call Dead Man's Curve, but few of them can live up to the reputation of State Route 125 between Amelia and Bethel, Ohio. This single stretch of road is thought by some to be the most haunted spot in Ohio. Without question, it is one of the most deadly.

State Route 125 began life as part of the original Ohio Turnpike. In 1831, when the road was built, this turnpike was one of the only roads through Ohio. As wagon and coach traffic increased, several small communities grew up along the new turnpike, including the village of Amelia, Ohio, (originally called Milltown or Milton) named in honor of a popular tollgate operator named Amerilous "Amelia" Bowdoin. Amelia's house still stands at 94 West Main Street, across the road from where it originally stood.

Amelia Bowdoin's House Today

Just south of Amelia, where State Route 125 intersects State Route 222, was once the location of a wicked bend in the road. From the very beginning, this sharp curve at the top of a steep hill became a death trap for unwary travelers who would sometimes slip over the edge. Even after the invention of the automobile when the road was modernized, many fatal accidents continued to occur on this part of the road, known today as Dead Man's Curve. There have been over seventy deaths here. In 2008, The General Health District of Clermont County listed State Route 125 between Amelia and Bethel as the #1 location for automobile accidents in the whole county.

In 1968, in an effort to make travel safer, the road was straightened and expanded. It was hoped that this major reconstruction project would bring an end to the infamous Dead Man's Curve but such was not the case. On October 19, 1969, only a month after reconstruction, it is said that a 1968 Impala carrying five teenagers was struck by a 1969 Roadrunner resulting in the deaths of all but one survivor, a man named Rick.

The Impala was believed to be traveling at over 100 miles per hour.

Since the day of this alleged accident in 1969, many frightened drivers have reported seeing a shadowy black apparition at Dead Man's Curve. People who have seen the dark figure up close say that it appears to have no face. This Faceless Hitchhiker is said to appear only between 1:20 and 1:40 in the morning and has been seen walking along the side of the road or sometimes crossing the road. It is claimed that the figure has even been known to throw rocks or to leap onto cars traveling through this intersection. Locals familiar with the legend try to avoid this part of highway when driving at night and those with psychic abilities will tell you that the whole area feels very evil and threatening.

In addition to the shadowy black figure, several people have reported seeing the Impala or Roadrunner from the accident in 1969, even though the actual cars are long gone. The cars appear to be moving or sometimes parked along the side of the road. These phantom cars are said to appear without drivers.

So why is Dead Man's Curve, now just an ordinary intersection, the most deadly spot in Clermont County? As far as I can determine, there is no rational explanation for this. The intersection seems completely benign. It certainly doesn't look unusually treacherous and the traffic here seems no more reckless than traffic on other parts of State Route 125. It is a common theory among many paranormal investigators that hauntings are likely to occur at places where Native American burial sites have been disturbed. If this is the case, the builders of the Ohio Turnpike may have stirred up paranormal activity when they cut through this part of Clermont County in 1831.

Dead Man's Curve lies on the very border of East Fork State Park, one of southwestern Ohio's largest recreational areas. Inside the park, behind a simple wooden fence, is an ancient burial mound known as Elk Lick Mound. No doubt, at one time there were other mounds and structural remains here. This is proof that in prehistoric times, people lived along the east fork of the Little Miami River. It is also strongly believed that a group of people from the Erie tribe settled in the area much later.

Elk Lick Mound

Like much of Ohio, from 800 BC to around 100 AD, this part of the county was populated by a prehistoric culture of Native Americans known as the Adena. The Adena people were farmers who built villages and planted crops such as sunflower and squash along the banks of Ohio's rivers and streams. They developed a rich culture, trading with other tribes and hunting and gathering Ohio's abundant supply of game and wild plants. They also seem to have developed a deeply spiritual relationship with all life and even the earth itself. Part of their spiritual life involved the building of small burial mounds. There were literally thousands of these mounds scattered throughout Ohio – more than any other state in the country. Today, most of these mounds have been completely obliterated by farming and development but about a hundred are being preserved in parks and on private land.

Around the year 100 AD, The Adena developed into the more advanced Hopewell culture. The Hopewell people also built mounds here as well as elaborate ceremonial earthworks, sacred ceremonial centers, and even circles of large standing stones very similar to those found in Great Britain. After the Hopewell culture collapsed around the year 400 AD, the Ohio valley went through a long period of isolation and cultural decline. For many hundreds of years the state was uninhabited and the true nature of its vanished prehistoric cultures was completely forgotten.

During this dark period, the few Native American hunting parties and European explorers coming into Ohio would have found the mounds and earthworks of earlier civilizations just as mysterious as we do today.

After the decline of the Hopewell culture, it is believed that some of the earliest Native Americans to migrate into southern Ohio were the Erie people who originally lived along the southern edge of Lake Erie, perhaps from present-day New York state to as far west as present-day Cleveland, Ohio. In 1575, a powerful confederation of tribes called the Iroquois Confederation was formed in central New York. This League of Five Nations – the Mohawks, Onondagas, Cayugas, Oneidas, and Sanecas, came to depend entirely on trade with the French, and later the English and Dutch. In exchange for beaver pelts, the Iroquois received essential goods such as guns and gunpowder, lead, knives, blankets, and metal cookware.

The Iroquois eventually wiped out the beaver population in their homeland and began encroaching on the lands of other Native tribes in Canada and the Ohio country. In 1649 a series of wars called the Beaver Wars broke out between the Iroquois Confederation and any tribe that would stand in their way. As the Iroquois spread westward along the southern shore of Lake Erie, tribe after tribe was defeated until only the Erie remained. Although they fought bravely, the Erie were eventually defeated and most of those who weren't killed were captured and either adopted into other tribes or enslaved.

But not all. Part of the Erie tribe managed to escape and it is thought that a small band of Erie people may have fled to the land in and around present-day East Fork State Park before they too died out or were assimilated into other tribes. In the 1700s other Native Americans began to migrate to parts of southern Ohio, followed by white settlers looking to carve their futures from its fertile ground.

To the Native Americans, burial sites and other religious sites will always be sacred, just as they were in the days of the Adena and Hopewell cultures. It is not surprising that they believed the ground here should be respected and left untouched. To disturb the burials or to remove artifacts from the ground is the worst kind of insult to its original inhabitants. Just as we try to protect and respect our cemeteries and sacred places today, Native Americans understandably believe their own burial sites and sacred places should be left to lie in peace, undisturbed.

**Old Bethel Methodist Church And Cemetery,
Inside East Fork State Park**

When white settlers settled here and began to build turnpikes, houses, and farms, they had little respect for the people who lived here before them and even less respect for their remains. Whether because of thoughtlessness or outright animosity, the land was completely and recklessly transformed to suit the new people streaming in to build their own homes, businesses, and places of worship. Sacred Native American sites were plowed under to plant crops, burial mounds and ceremonial earthworks were destroyed, and the artifacts were plucked from their resting places, collected and sold to museums or private collectors.

There is very little left to remind us of earlier Native cultures, before European settlers moved west into the new American frontier. All that remain are a few mounds of earth and some artifacts salvaged from the ground. And perhaps spirits.

I visited East Fork State Park for the first time on March 8, 2009. My parents were with me and we had decided to explore the park and take a few photos. It was a beautiful warm and sunny day. As we drove down to see the lake, my mom started feeling very uneasy. She is a sensitive and can often pick up on the unusual paranormal energy of a location, if there is any. As soon as we pulled into the parking area in front of the lake, she said, "I don't like this place. Let's go. I don't like it here." There was no obvious reason to feel apprehensive about the location. It looked perfectly fine to me, but I've come to trust my mom's feelings about this kind of thing so I immediately turned the car around and left the area. As soon as we lost sight of the lake, Mom felt better. I asked her what she thought it was about the lake that bothered her and she said, "There are dead people under that water."

East Fork Lake is not a natural formation. It was created in 1978 when the U.S. Army Corps of Engineers built a dam, flooding the Little Miami River basin as part of their flood control program. With 32.4 miles of shoreline and 1,971 acres of surface area, the lake provides visitors to East Fork State Park with a prime place for fishing and boating.

What really lies beneath the water? In prehistoric times, the Adena people certainly lived in this part of Clermont County and a small portion of the Erie tribe probably lived here much later so if these people lived right here, it stands to reason that they also died and were buried here.

Even though a tiny part of Adena culture has been preserved within the park, the land has been desecrated in many ways. In

1869, two gold mines operated in the vicinity. Surely, flooding the land, building roads, and digging mines was a disruption to the land's sacred properties. When I visited Elk Lick Mound, I saw that someone had tossed a plastic bottle onto the top of the mound, demonstrating to me that people today are as thoughtless as ever. Could this blatant disrespect for ancient civilizations and sacred burial ground be the reason there have been so many deaths at Dead Man's Curve? Some people believe so.

Abandoned House On Bantam Road

What about that faceless hitchhiker people claim to see? If the reports are true, could it be the ghost of one of the many people who have died in traffic accidents at Dead Man's Curve? Or is the black faceless form some manifestation of the resentment the sacred land itself has produced? If you believe that the earth has paranormal properties of its own, this is another possibility. If the land isn't cursed, it is at least unappreciated from a historical perspective. Perhaps the landscape is holding the spirits of those who have died here from prehistoric times up to the present day.

People still claim to see the ghosts of those two cars involved in a deadly collision on Dead Man's Curve back in 1969 and they still tell stories of a faceless shadow figure. Whether or not you believe the stories, the fact remains that this simple intersection is part of the most deadly stretch of road in Clermont County.

Another View Of Dead Man's Curve

DIRECTIONS: Although the original Dead Man's Curve is long gone, it was once located in the area where State Route 125 intersects State Route 222 in Clermont County between Amelia and Bethel, Ohio. State Route 125 turns into Bantam Road to the east where it leads to an entrance to East Fork State Park.

Buffalo Ridge

Buffalo Ridge Road is a hilly roller coaster of a road located just outside of Cleves, Ohio in Colerain Township. I have lived in Colerain Township for all but a few years of my life and for as long as I can remember, I have heard about Buffalo Ridge and the paranormal dangers lurking there. If you believe the stories, there are a vast number of scary things just waiting to pounce on you.

In our high school newspaper, I recall a story about a guy named Meat Cleaver Charlie, a naked man with a meat cleaver who would come running out at you if you dared to cross his path. Other legends sprang up over the years, such as a story of a headless bride and other ghosts who could be seen wandering the road. Other people claimed to see a phantom dog with glowing green eyes. But wait, there's more! How about some Satan worshipers lurking around an old abandoned crematorium? Or the sounds of a ghost car drifting over the hills, said to be the victims of a gang initiation gone wrong? How about an old abandoned house with a witch in the window? Or mysterious ghostly fog? Or the bloody stain left by a boy killed while riding his bicycle in nearby Mitchell Memorial Forest?

Just when you think that your credibility has been stretched to the limit, you hear another legend. And another. The stories about Buffalo Ridge have become so unbelievably bizarre, it would seem that not even the most naive school children would believe them. And yet, they do and the same stories seem to circulate year after year.

Most of the legends seem to center around an old crematorium allegedly located back in the woods, somewhere off of Buffalo Ridge. Some people say the crematorium mysteriously blew up.

Amazingly, the place is real! However, I am sorry to say it isn't an abandoned crematorium, as most people believe. And no, it isn't an abandoned planetarium, as recorded in some books and videos. And no, it didn't even blow up. In truth, if you dare to visit this site, you will see the ruins of what was supposed to have been an ordinary astronomical observatory. Here is what really happened.

From 1896 to 1910, Dr. Delisle Stewart served as an assistant astronomer at the Cincinnati Observatory of the University of Cincinnati. The observatory did not have an astrophotography program at the time and Stewart tried to persuade his director to apply this new photographic technology to their work at the Cincinnati Observatory. Regrettably, Dr. Stewart's persistence cost him his job. His response was to create a new astronomical society, dedicated to astrophotographic research.

Dr. Stewart named his new society the Cincinnati Astronomical Society, a name borrowed from the original organization in existence from 1845 to 1870.

Cincinnati Chamber Of Commerce Building *

Just as Dr. Stewart was looking for the means to provide his new society with an observatory, a catastrophe struck Cincinnati's Chamber of Commerce building. On January 10, 1911, the beautiful building was gutted by fire with a loss of six lives. Designed by world-famous architect Henry Hobson Richardson, it was was the pride of Cincinnati and featured on postcards of the time. Seeing a good opportunity, Stewart planned to build his new observatory based on the architectural plan of the Chamber of Commerce building and to use its salvaged granite blocks to face the walls of the observatory. For this observatory, they planned to build on Buffalo Ridge, a site chosen because of its distance (about 20 miles) from Cincinnati, making it a great place to observe and photograph the night sky.

Within three years, citizens had donated enough money to buy 142 acres of land for the observatory's construction and to move the blocks from downtown Cincinnati to a temporary storage location, and finally to the building site on Buffalo Ridge. These massive granite blocks weighed as much as 27,500 pounds and moving them was an expensive venture. By the time the blocks were transported all the way up to Buffalo Ridge, the Cincinnati Astronomical Society had completely run out of money.

For the next twenty years, Dr. Stewart begged the people of Cincinnati for more money. At the end of the 1930s, after what must have seemed like an eternity, enough funds were raised to begin the actual construction of the observatory. An ambitious project from the beginning, the two-story observatory would have been impressive. It was going to feature a large central dome with two side domes, offices, a library, a museum of astronomy, a reception hall, lecture hall, classrooms, photographic darkrooms, and more. The observatory's domes were going to house three large telescopes. Richardson's stones salvaged from the Chamber of Commerce building in Cincinnati would then be used as facing on the outside of the observatory.

Disastrously, after finishing just the basic outline of the building and a basement area, the Great Depression hit the country and funding once again ran dry. Lacking the money to complete the observatory, the society was forced to abandon the project once and for all. The basement area, constructed of concrete blocks, is all that remains of the observatory project.

Granite Blocks Scattered Everywhere

In March 2009, my dad and I decided to investigate the site of this unfinished observatory. As we followed the trail back into the woods, weeds and vines clung to my legs, causing me to stumble a few times. There were a few trees down, blocking the way, but after walking for a hundred yards or so we came to what is left of Dr. Delisle Stewart's uncompleted observatory. Sinking into a deep pit is the basement area and what looks like it was going to be one of the domes. There are other trails going off in all directions, leading to fields filled with granite blocks. There doesn't seem to be any pattern to the scattered piles, leading me to believe the tremendously heavy blocks were just dumped without any regard for their intended purpose. There are blocks everywhere and it is easy to see how someone would believe this was once a building destroyed by a great explosion.

More Ruins From The Unfinished Observatory

More Ruins From The Unfinished Observatory

I didn't see any obvious evidence of Satanic activity but I did see quite a few beer bottles and lots of trash. Since the days when this construction project came to an end, I imagine there have been countless young people coming out here to drink. Perhaps to scare each other with stories of ghostly mists, devil dogs, headless brides, and other terrible phantoms of Buffalo Ridge. There are even rumors that this area was the childhood playground of the infamous Charles Manson. I don't know what evidence there is to prove this. I do know that Charles Manson was born in Cincinnati but what childhood he had was spent in other places, far away from Buffalo Ridge. Still, Manson is everybody's favorite creepy character and I guess if you are going to make up an urban legend, it's not a bad idea to throw his name into it for some dramatic flair.

Mitchell Memorial Forest borders Buffalo Ridge Road, so while in the area, I tried to find that stain left by the boy who had been struck by a car. Like most legendary stains, it was supposed to be one of those stains that would never wash away, so I figured I had a good chance of finding it. "I'm looking for mysterious stains" didn't seem to impress the employee working at the park entrance when I visited Mitchell Memorial Forest the previous year, but I thought I would try again. No luck. Mitchell Memorial Forest is a nice place though. This 1,336-acre park has a nature trail, playground for the kids, a pond, a stone memorial shelter, and even a 4-mile mountain bike trail (which they are very proud of). The park was made possible by land donated by Morris Mitchell who donated the land as a memorial to his parents.

The Present-day Cincinnati Astronomical Society

After the death of its founder, Dr. Stewart, the Cincinnati Astronomical Society became an amateur astronomy group. The club's headquarters is now located directly across the street from Mitchell Memorial Forest on Zion Road. They use this facility to hold monthly meetings and to promote a greater understanding of astronomy. Although they never got their own observatory, the group has managed to survive.

Not all of the stones from the ruins of the Cincinnati Chamber of Commerce Building were left to languish on Buffalo Ridge. You can find these distinctive pink granite blocks in some of the strangest places. In 1972, architecture students from the University of Cincinnati used 84 tons of its stones to create a memorial dedicated to H.H. Richardson, the building's famous architect. This memorial is located in Burnet Woods, directly across the street from the University of Cincinnati.

Two Views Of The H.H. Richardson Memorial, Cincinnati

Two of the carved stones can be found at the Farbach-Werner Nature Preserve in Colerain Township where they are being used as decorative elements for the park's butterfly garden.

More Stones At Farbach-Werner Nature Preserve

So what about all of those ghosts and legends? According to people living on Buffalo Ridge Road and in the surrounding area, there is nothing supernatural here. Still, that doesn't seem to stop people who continue to drive up and down the mountainous road, looking for thrills. I've driven over Buffalo Ridge quite a few times and I have never seen a headless bride, a dog with glowing green eyes, or any of the other legendary wandering ghouls said to be here. The road is very cavernous and surrounded by thick woods. It can be a creepy place at night, if you are not familiar with the area, but that certainly doesn't make it haunted.

Several people have claimed that if you drive at night on Buffalo Ridge, you will be chased away by a black van, a white van, or a truck. Usually these vehicles are described as having tinted windows. If anything "chases" you, it will probably belong to the Hamilton County Park District. I know that people living on the road are sick and tried of seeing strangers race up and down the road at night to hunt for ghosts and spooky creatures. I imagine that if I lived there, I would want to chase people away too.

Some Not-So-Mysterious White Park Vehicles

Make up anything you like and it couldn't be more preposterous than the stories already associated with Buffalo Ridge. I can't say if this road is really haunted but as far as I can tell, none of the popular legends are based in fact, leaving me to have my doubts. I truly believe that if you brought a truckload of ghost-hunting equipment and a dozen psychics to Buffalo Ridge, you would find nothing but stories and rumors. And maybe a few aggravated park rangers.

DIRECTIONS: Buffalo Ridge is located near Cleves, Ohio. Take East Miami River Road west from Cleves, turn left onto Gum Run Road which will lead up to Buffalo Ridge Road. Turn right onto Buffalo Ridge Road and then left on Zion Road to reach Mitchell Memorial Forest.

Rapid Run Park

Rapid Run Park in the Price Hill area of Cincinnati is a city park covering almost fifty acres. Entering the park from the parking lot on Rapid Run Pike, you walk along a paved pathway leading around a small pond surrounded by a large open grassy area. This main section of the park is backed up against a high ridge and at the top of the ridge is a stone picnic shelter with sets of swings on either side. At the back of the park is a wooded section, with Guerley Road bordering the park just behind. On the opposite side of Rapid Run Pike are a couple of baseball fields.

Originally called Lick Run Park, most of the land was acquired between 1928-1930 with one parcel of Potter's Field property obtained by ordinance in 1934. At first, the primitive park was long neglected. No improvements were made until 1941 when the WPA constructed roadways, a pond, pathways, picnic facilities, and the stone shelter. It then reopened in 1942.

It all looks very peaceful and quiet now but there is something about the park that seems sinister. When people visit, they stay far apart as if trying to avoid contact. The few times I have explored the area, the playgrounds have been empty. The stone shelter was also vacant. You can feel a sense of loneliness permeating the atmosphere here, even on a warm summer day.

It doesn't surprise me that there are rumors and reports of several ghosts said to be haunting the park. At the swing set on the west side of the shelter, people have reported seeing ghostly children playing and they have heard giggling when there were no living children around. Some have actually seen the center swing move by itself as if an invisible child was playing there. Other people claim to have seen the ghost of a small boy or girl, apparently five or six years old. Still other people have reported seeing ghostly shapes moving along the path at the top of the ridge near a trail leading through the woods to Guerley Road.

Empty Swings On East Side Of Rapid Run Park

If Rapid Run Park is haunted, it has a good excuse. The park is surrounded by death. Schachnus Cemetery, Montefiore Cemetery, and the United Jewish Cemetery all lie just to the northeast and the park itself is built over the site of one of Cincinnati's largest Potter's Fields.

This old Potter's Field, a 25-acre cemetery, is where up to 11,000 of Cincinnati's poor and forgotten were laid to rest. Many of these people died at The Branch Hospital for Contagious Diseases (eventually renamed the Dunham Tuberculosis Hospital), which was located nearby on a hill just up Guerley Road. Although the hospital was considered to be one of the best in the country at the time, there was no cure for tuberculosis and attempts to treat the disease were highly experimental, painful, and ineffectual. Thousands who died here were carried down the hill and hastily buried in a cemetery of unmarked graves.

The first time I tried to find this cemetery, if you can even call it that, I had to drive up and down the road several times before I found it. I asked a jogger, out for his morning run, and he told me he had never heard of a Potter's Field. Apparently, even people living here are unaware of their neighborhood's history. Abandoned now and overgrown with weeds, the site is difficult to find. If you look along Gurley Road, you will see a very small sign at the edge of someone's driveway. The sign reads:

"This 25 acre cemetery is the former burial site for Hamilton County's poor, unwanted, and unknown. Established in 1849 and operated until 1981, between 8,500 and 10,000 people are laid to rest here. Most of the graves are unmarked but some have metal plates or wooden stakes marking the burial site. A veteran's section was set aside and many Civil War soldiers are believed to be buried here. Records of known graves were recorded in a book kept by the County Department of Human Resources. There are no written records of burials before 1898. The Branch Hospital for Contagious Diseases, locally referred to as the "Pest House" controlled the cemetery from 1879 to 1912. The hospital was located at the site of what is now the Dunham Recreation Center. Persons who died at the "Pest House" were buried here as quickly as possible, foregoing customary funeral services. The Hamilton County Welfare Department eventually took over operations of the cemetery after the hospital closed. In order to preserve

and protect the many graves, known and unknown, and the growth that has occurred over the passing years, Potter's Field is now being maintained in a natural state."

By "natural state" I suppose they mean an impassible thicket of gnarly weeds. I tried to push my way back into the cemetery to see if I could find any of the grave markers, but couldn't get very far because the area is so overgrown, it is impossible to see anything. Supposedly, somewhere among these weeds are thousands of unmarked graves, as well as a few with broken grave markers.

An older metal plaque at the border of the Potter's Field reads:

"Potter's Field, 1849 – Public Burial Place For Those Who Have No One To Provide For Their Burial. The Original Potter's Field Was Bought With The Thirty Pieces Of Silver Which Judas Was Paid To Betray Jesus. His Guilt Was So Great, He Hung Himself On A Judas Tree, Known In Our Country As A Red-Bud Tree."

In the 1980s, Charlie Luken, the former mayor of Cincinnati, fought for the city to maintain this field by at least mowing it, but the cost to taxpayers was considered to be too high and so it was left as we see it today – a patch of weeds on the side of the road. The whole Potter's Field area is now ignored and forgotten, along with those who are buried here.

Lone Swing On The West Side Of The Shelter

Few people are aware of it but across the road, hidden beneath the scenic tranquility of Rapid Run Park, were more unmarked graves. When WPA workers dug up the ground in the 1940s to create the pond in the center of the park, they unearthed the bones of several bodies. No one knows what happened to these bodies but if the very center of the park contained unmarked graves, it is fairly certain that there were many more. Some may still be there under the grass, under the playgrounds, and under the pathways.

I first investigated Rapid Run Park a couple of times in 2007, taking EMF readings, making digital recordings in the hopes of capturing some EVP, and taking dozens of photographs. I didn't detect anything I would call paranormal, but as it is with all haunted places, timing is everything. I may have been there at the wrong time. There was a single swing on one of the swing sets, hanging motionless and dejected. Is this the swing people have seen moving by itself? There were no signs of children, living or dead.

Inside the park's shelter, I was baffled to find a rope hanging from a rafter in the center. It was cut at the end and directly beneath the rope was an odd burnt spot. It didn't appear to be ashes from a wood fire. It looked more like something had melted into a blob. The burnt spot and rope both appeared to be fairly new. What was this? Was it some kind of bizarre barbecue rig? Obviously something had been suspended from the rope and burned, but what? And why? What was that stuff on the floor? I can't say for sure that the shelter was anything other than uncomfortable, but it doesn't surprise me to hear that spirits have allegedly been seen here too.

Cut Rope And Strange Residue Inside The Shelter

To me, it seems likely that the children who died at the tuberculosis hospital nearby and who are buried in unmarked graves beneath the park may have a reason to haunt the area. A playground would be an attractive sight to any child. Could it be that the poor forgotten children are coming here to play? Are they trying to recapture some of the lives they missed by passing away before their time? Without a doubt, the children and adults who lived and died at the tuberculosis hospital suffered greatly before they passed away. Having your body dumped into an unmarked grave is not a respectful way to go. No funeral. No one to remember you. No one to mourn your death.

It is no wonder that Rapid Run Park has a strange feel to it. After being used for so many years as a place to dump the unwanted dead from nearby hospitals, most especially the tuberculosis hospital on the hill, the park seems more like a memorial to the dead than a place of recreation for the living.

Branch Hospital For Contagious Diseases *

The history of the tuberculosis hospital is murky, due in part to the many name changes it went through over the years. Starting out as the Branch Hospital for Contagious Diseases, it later became the Cincinnati Tubercular (or Tuberculosis) Hospital, then the Hamilton County Tuberculosis Sanatorium, and the name was finally changed to the Dunham Tuberculosis Hospital in 1945 until it closed.

According to early descriptions of the original 150-acre complex, there was a main hospital located on a hill in the center of the grounds, surrounded by other buildings such as a nurses' home, garage, occupational therapy building, dormitories for the staff, and a Preventorium used for treatments to prevent tuberculosis. The Preventorium contained a children's school operated by the Board of Education. There were also tents and small buildings called Sunshine Cottages where some tuberculosis patients were kept, the idea being that the sunlight would be therapeutic. The main hospital had a bed capacity of 583 with an additional 100 beds in the Preventorium.

Children Attending Open-Air Classroom At Branch Hospital *

The old hospital complex is still there on the hill overlooking Rapid Run Park. It has been transformed into the Dunham Recreation Center which opened in 1973. The 80-acre complex now features a fitness center, gym, game room, theater, wading pool, golf course and other recreational facilities for people of all ages. The hospital building itself is now home to the Sunset Players, a local theatrical group. The Preventorium, once full of children, is used to hold community workshops.

Present-Day Dunham Recreation Center

Sunshine Cottage At Branch Hospital *

Is Rapid Run Park haunted as people claim? I didn't find any evidence to support this idea but I am going to have to say it is a real possibility, due to the nature of the area. As you walk the grounds of Rapid Run Park, you should remember that the people who are (or were) buried in the ground beneath your feet all died horrible and tragic deaths. Those who didn't die at the tuberculosis hospital up the street were transferred here from other hospitals to be disposed of like trash. Covered up, nameless, and forgotten, they never really got the respectful goodbye they deserved and now even the Potter's Field where most of them are buried has been overrun by weeds. I believe that if restless spirits are capable of haunting anything, Rapid Run Park would be a prime location.

DIRECTIONS: Rapid Run Park is located at 4450 Rapid Run Parkway in Cincinnati. To reach the Dunham Recreation Center, take Dunham Way off of Guerley Road on the northwestern side of Rapid Run Park. Dunham Way forks into two Dunham Lanes leading to various parts of the complex of buildings.

DO NOT visit Rapid Run Park by yourself and never go at night. This is a city park and unfortunately it is a high-crime area. There are occasional shootings and the day after my last visit, there was an attempted kidnapping at the park, so be careful.

Tiny Town

Not long ago, this dark valley held a strange collection of buildings. It looked like an 18th century frontier town, complete with a miniature blockhouse and structures made of stucco, rough-hewn logs, and rocks. The buildings, scattered along the hillside, were painted white with brightly colored yellow and red symbols. A few electric lights barely lit the scene. A creek that ran along the entire border seemed like a moat and the blockhouse straddled the creek, serving as the town's main entrance. Would-be intruders, beware.

A frontier town would have been a strange enough sight in present-day Ohio but there was something else about this place. It was just too small. The buildings seemed to be one third the size of normal houses and shelters. There were smoke stacks, fire pits, and signs of life. This wasn't just some kind of historic reconstruction. It was a real place with real houses and real people. But who lived here?

Over the years, people came to believe that Tiny Town, or Munchkinland as it came to be called, was populated by a commune of munchkins. A bizarre band of little people who had come to this valley to escape the prying eyes of strangers. Or maybe they were a band of little people who had run away from the circus. Supposedly, if you drove past Tiny Town late at night, the residents would come running out to chase you away. Screaming in their shrill little voices, shaking their fists, running out at you and throwing rocks. This was their town. Their refuge. And they didn't like visitors. The place certainly looked scary enough on moonless nights or when the fog moved in. Some people used to say you could hear the faint sounds of circus music coming from inside the buildings, If you were brave, you could ring a large bell at the edge of town and then run for your life, hoping to make it back to the safety of your car before the angry munchkins caught you. Your friends would scream and later you could enjoy a good laugh, knowing that you had escaped the freakish place.

The Blockhouse

The truth is, what some people believed to be a town of little people was actually a place called Handlebar Ranch. Anna and

Percy Ritter bought the land in 1940 and soon started a small business renting bicycles. In later years, the Ritters started a hayride business and built these small houses and picnic shelters in order to provide a central location for the business. Handlebar Ranch operated for many years, renting hayride wagons as well as hosting parties and picnics.

Bicycles For Rent - Handlebar Ranch In The Early Days *

Over the years, Anna and Percy were constantly tormented by teenagers and drunks who would vandalize the property or cruise up and down the road at all hours in search of munchkins.

Sadly, Anna and Percy Ritter have both passed away. Anna passed away in February 2007 and in November 2008 the entire property was purchased by the Rumpke waste disposal company. The ranch, Anna's house, and all surrounding structures were quickly bulldozed to the ground. Rumpke dump, the region's only waste disposal site (and the tallest point in Hamilton County), takes in 7,500 – 8,000 tons of trash per day and it will only be a matter of time before the property formerly known as Handlebar Ranch is buried forever beneath the debris. Since Tiny Town is gone forever, I am including a series of photos I took at the site on September 10, 2007 before it was destroyed:

Headless Brides and Devil Dogs

Headless Brides and Devil Dogs

The Ritters' home was up a steep hill, within a compound of buildings across the road from Handlebar Ranch.

The buildings of Tiny Town were covered with colorful Native American icons and characters. On the side of this building are depicted Kokopelli Katsina (a respected spirit) and a Tlingit Warrior. The figure below resembles a Hopi snake dancer. The spiral may represent a journey or water, since Tiny Town was located next to a creek.

2008, shortly after the Rumpke company bought the property and bulldozed everything to the ground.

2008, After The Destruction Of Tiny Town

DIRECTIONS: Now that the ranch has been destroyed, hardly anything remains of Tiny Town but you can see what's left of it if you drive down Hughes Road (between Bank and Struble Roads) in Colerain Township. Look on the west side of the road, bordered by a creek.

There is a ridge that used to mark the edge of Tiny Town and you can probably still see the rocks lining a creek on the side of the road. On the opposite side of Hughes road is where the Ritter home used to stand.

Hangman's Hollow

There are a few variations of the legend of Hangman's Hollow but the most reliable version is based on a true story published in the Hamilton Telegraph on October 13, 1910.

According to this account, four men from the small village of Darrtown (just north of Hamilton, Ohio) traveled by horseback to Hamilton to spend the day at the Butler County Fair. This was Butler County's first state-sponsored fair, held October 2-3, 1851 at a site east of Hamilton, along High Street and east of Fifth Street.

Taylor Marshall, Ben Scott, Chambers Flenner, and Dan Harwick would have spent the day looking at the horses, cattle, swine, collections of fabrics, and other articles, as well as enjoying some good food and maybe a drink or two. After a long day at the fair, the four men mounted their horses and started back to Darrtown.

Traveling west for about a mile or so along what is now called Main Street or Hamilton-Richmond Road, they came to a hollow in the road. It was starting to get dark by this time, but off to the side of the road they could see a small group of people who all seemed to be looking at something. Slowing down to take a look, the men coming from the fair noticed a dead man hanging from a tree. It appeared as though the man had been dead for several days.

Strangely, the man was hanged with his own suspenders. No one knew for sure whether it had been murder or suicide, but murders weren't uncommon along Ohio's dusty turnpikes in those days. The dead man was later identified as a livestock dealer who had last been seen in Hamilton about a week earlier and was known to have been doing business with farmers in Butler County. Some say he had been flashing around a big roll of cash. He had left a local hotel about a week earlier and never returned.

After satisfying their curiosity, the fair goers made their way back home and the grisly scene was forgotten. But then the legend began.

Soon after the night of the hanging, people began to see a mysterious shadowy figure in the ravine, believed to be the ghost of the stockman. Others reported hearing creepy voices coming from the woods. Some of the voices seemed to be trying to warn travelers of danger lurking in the darkness ahead. For years after the hanging, people would hurry their horses in order to pass as quickly as possible along this part of the road. Turning their heads at every little sound, sure that the ghosts of the hollow were following close behind.

What became known as Hangman's Hollow was described in the earliest accounts as "a cavernous ravine which looked impenetrable in its abysmal recess." This dip in the road was surrounded by deep woods and looked to be a sinister tunnel through the tall trees overhead.

I have investigated Hangman's Hollow several times with EMF detectors, night vision equipment, voice recorders, and other equipment, but heavy traffic in the area prevents me from doing a proper investigation. Hangman's Hollow is no longer the lonely wooded place it was in 1851, and if there are any ghostly voices in the woods, they are being drowned out by the sound of passing cars and trucks.

Hangman's Hollow – Main Street, Looking South

Taylor Marshall, Ben Scott, Chambers Flenner, and Dan Harwick did see the hanged man on the side of the road, according to the newspaper article from 1910, but was there ever a haunting in the woods at Hangman's Hollow? What about the eerie voices and apparitions seen in the area? Were people really experiencing these things or were they just frightened by a bizarre death and the dark sinister woods? It's impossible to tell after all of these years.

The hollow is still there, if you care to visit it yourself, though it may be difficult to recognize after so much development. What little is left of Hangman's Hollow lies just northwest of the intersection of Old Oxford Road, Gardner Road, and Hamilton-Richmond Road (also called Main or Route 177). These three roads connect in a patch of woods. No doubt, the tree where they found the hanged man is long gone but if you look closely, you may be able to see a dip in the landscape - the infamous haunted woods.

The village of Darrtown is also still there, north of Hamilton. It was named after Conrad Darr who came from Pennsylvania and laid out the original village on April 4, 1814. Darr had purchased the land for $1.25 an acre and soon started the town's first inn, called The Hitching Post. His inn was a popular stop for travelers on the Hamilton-Fairborn stagecoach line. People could stop at the inn for a free drink or get a gallon of whiskey for fifty cents a gallon, provided they brought their own jug. Seventy five cents a gallon if Mr. Darr provided the jug. He died on July 4, 1852 and is buried in Darrtown Cemetery, located on Shollenbarger Road, one mile west of Darrtown.

Abandoned House On Darrtown Road

DIRECTIONS: Hangman's Hollow lies between Hamilton and Darrtown, Ohio. Old Oxford Road, Gardner Road, and Hamilton-Richmond Road come together here to form a Y at the point where the legend is supposed to have originated. The area is built up now with stores, gas stations, and banks but strangely enough there is still a single wooded area - a reminder of how Hangman's Hollow once appeared.

The Oxford Motorcycle

Sometimes called the Oxford Light or the Oxford Motorcycle Light, this mystery has been around for decades. Literally hundreds of people have seen the light but exactly what causes it, no one knows.

According to legend, a young man intended to take his motorcycle to his girlfriend's house so that he could propose marriage. Riding north on Oxford-Milford Road, just outside of Oxford, he came to the sharp bend in the road, lost control of his motorcycle, and was decapitated by a barbed wire fence. He almost made it. His girlfriend allegedly lived just around the bend, on Earhart Road.

Other versions of this legend claim the motorcycle rider died when he hit an oncoming car or tractor. Another version says that he collided with a bicycle. This version of the legend has splintered into a separate legend, claiming that a boy on a bicycle haunts nearby Buckley Road.

Still another version of the Oxford Motorcycle legend says that there was a serial rapist on the loose. One night he approached a home on Earhart Road and knocked on a girl's door. Fearing for her safety, the girl called her boyfriend who rushed to her rescue. Unfortunately, the boy's motorcycle crashed when he tried to make the sharp turn in the road.

Now people allege to see the lights of that motorcycle, even though the motorcycle and rider are long gone. If you drive north to the sharp 90-degree bend where Oxford-Milford Road becomes Earhart Road and face south, turn off the car's engine, flash your headlights three times and wait, you will see a light approach from the opposite direction. They say you will see this white light move north along the side of Oxford-Milford Road, and then it will disappear just as it reaches you. Some people even claim to see a red light they believe to be the phantom motorcycle's taillight.

The problem with the legend of the crashed motorcycle rider is that longtime residents in the area insist they have never heard of such an accident. In 1992, William Falk (a man who lived in the house where the girl supposedly lived) had never even heard the story, even though he was 70 years old and had always lived in the same house.

On the surface, this legend sounds like dozens of other legends you may have heard before. Natives of Ohio may think it sounds remarkably similar to the legend of the Elmore Rider. According to the Elmore Rider legend, a man was recently discharged from the army and after mounting his motorcycle he rode off to find his old girlfriend. When he arrived, he discovered that she had become engaged to another man. The distraught man then roared off, lost control of his motorcycle at a point where the road curved and crossed a bridge, and just like the poor guy from Oxford, he crashed through a barbed wire fence and lost his head.

Now every March 21st, the anniversary of the Elmore Rider's death, people come from all around, hoping to see him at the haunted bridge. And just like the Oxford Motorcycle, people try to coax the ghost into view by flashing their headlights three times or blowing their car horns three times. Elmore is a small town southeast of Toledo and east of Bowling Green University. The bridge where the rider is reported to appear is east of Elmore at a place where it crosses the middle branch of the Portage River.

Dozens of people have written to tell me they have seen the Oxford Motorcycle Light. So many people travel out to the site, it has become a real nuisance to people living in the area. A retired policeman told me he has seen the light himself on two different occasions, on two separate sections of the road. Other police officers have seen the light as well. In fact, it seems that anyone who bothers to go there will see this light. Some have reported seeing it many times.

Looking East, Where The Curve Becomes Earhart Road

So what is it? Many people have tried to find out what is causing the light, but so far they have failed. Phantom motorcycle or not, it is just one of those things that can't be explained.

I first looked for the Oxford Motorcycle on January 21, 2009. Although it wasn't quite dark yet, I parked at the bend in the road where Oxford-Milford Road becomes Earhart Road, faced the car south, and set up my camcorder on a tripod. I flashed the car's headlights three times and waited. And waited. Nothing abnormal appeared, Maybe because it wasn't dark yet. I have no idea. Oxford-Milford Road is a very long and very straight stretch of road. All along the road, it dips up and down considerably as it passes through hilly farmland. If you watch carefully, you can see cars miles away. They seem to disappear and then reappear as they come over the long road. When they turn off onto driveways or intersecting roads, the cars disappear from view.

If a car suddenly pulled onto another road or into a driveway, it would explain how a car's headlights would suddenly seem to disappear but it does nothing to explain why so many people claim to see a light travel all the way up the road and then disappear right in front of their eyes just as it reaches them. And there's another thing to consider – most people say they see the light travel from south to north but some people have reported seeing the light traveling north to south and can see it from the opposite end of the road, as far south as Somerville Road. People see the light but never see a car or motorcycle attached to it. Nothing but a light bouncing along, straight up the contour of the road.

People have been seeing strange lights like this for hundreds of years. In some places they are called spook lights. Other people have called them will-o-the-wisps or fee fo lais. However, these types of lights are usually associated with damp swampy ground, nothing like the farmland you find at the Oxford Motorcycle location.

If there were something here, why on earth would it perform on cue every time someone flashes their car's headlights three times? And why does the light fade out just before it reaches you? And why does the light seem to travel straight up the road?

I have been back to the spot a couple more times, day and night, but I have yet to see anything unusual. Apparently, I am the only person who hasn't seen this ghost motorcycle. Just my luck.

As far as I can tell, there is nothing in the area but houses and farmland. It would be interesting to find out if there was ever a cemetery or church located at the bend in the road where the light seems to disappear. In Europe, before the days of modern funerals and hearses, they used to build long straight roads connecting churches and cemeteries. Called "corpse roads," "church paths," or "ghost roads," these long straight roads were used to carry the dead to their burial places. For some people, this involved carrying the body by hand or by horseback, often for long distances over difficult terrain. It was believed by many people that ghosts would travel these paths at night, traveling very close to the ground, from one cemetery to the next or from church to cemetery. These ghost roads were avoided at night and German folklore maintained that these roads took on the "magical characteristics of the dead" and should not be obstructed in any way.

In Britain, there is an old custom called the "church porch watch" or "sitting up" in which people who were spiritually sensitive would hold a vigil between 11:00 PM and 1:00 AM at a graveyard or ghost road. These special people would watch the road or graveyard for the specters of those who would die within the next year. Usually these vigils took place at times when the veil between the world of the living and the world of the dead was very thin – Saint Mark's Eve (April 24th), Halloween, New Year's Eve, Midsummer, or Christmas. Traditionally, these doomed souls could be seen traveling up the ghost road to the cemetery or church door. Maybe these special times of the year would be good times to watch for the Oxford Motorcycle, if it actually exists.

Is Oxford-Milford Road somehow taking on "magical characteristics of the dead" as people used to believe? Was the story of the Oxford Motorcycle just fabricated in order to explain some sort of bizarre natural phenomenon in the area? Is it all just a weird optical illusion? Whether you look at it from a scientific point of view or from a more traditional spiritual view, I don't think we have a solid answer yet. You can either choose to believe there is nothing here and that hundreds of people have fooled themselves into seeing what they want to see or else you can check it out for yourself and try to find the truth. So far, we have no real evidence unless you count a lot of videos shot by jumpy squealing college kids who never seem to get out of their cars.

I'm sorry to say it, but my guess is that this light is only an optical illusion which has given birth to a popular legend with no basis in fact. When you are sitting at the bend in the road, you can look south and see for at least a mile. At night, cars coming up the road appear clearly but since they are so far away, their two headlights seem to be one. It is very easy to fool yourself into thinking the car is a motorcycle, even if it isn't, and it is impossible to judge distance at night. You can't really tell how far away the cars are.

I have seen numerous videos of the "Oxford Light" and none of them show the light actually coming anywhere near the person with the camcorder. Optically, it seems to get closer but it is still far away and never really reaches the viewer. All a car has to do is turn into a driveway or onto one of the side roads off of Oxford-Milford Road and the car will seem to disappear.

Until someone gets a video or even a good still photograph of a light up close, with no car, truck, or motorcycle attached, I'm going to say this is only an optical illusion and nothing more, especially since there has never been a fatal motorcycle accident on this section of the road.

DIRECTIONS: Take Trenton-Oxford Road (Rt. 73) east out of Oxford, then take a left onto Oxford-Milford Road. Go straight until you come to a 90-degree curve in the road. This is where Oxford-Milford Road turns into Earhart Road. Turn the car around to face south on Oxford-Milford. Be extremely careful and do not trespass onto private property. Local residents are very tired of people stopping here to look for ghost motorcycles and the police WILL ask you to leave. Especially on weekends.

Pond Run Road

Pond Run Road in New Richmond, Ohio is purportedly the home of the infamous Hook Man. Our local version, at least. A modern bridge now stands where an old wooden bridge used to exist. Supposedly, this wooden bridge was once a popular place for young people to hang out and get friendly with each other. There are no places for you to pull over now, but the legends are still being passed along.

If you've ever seen a horror movie or read a scary novel, you've probably heard some version of the Hook Man legend. According to the people of New Richmond, their very own Hook Man can be found near this bridge on Pond Run Road.

The legend maintains that there was once a family living in the area and they had a boy who had a bad temper and didn't play well with others, so the parents kept him close to home. Sometimes, to avoid confrontations, they would chain the boy up in the basement. One stormy night, lightning struck the house and set the house ablaze. While the parents were overcome and died from the smoke, the boy miraculously broke his bounds and escaped, but at the expense of one of his hands. And then of course the boy found a hook somewhere and used it as a hand, thus becoming the dreaded Hook Man of Pond Run Road, wandering through the woods and terrifying teenagers forever more.

People say the old wooden bridge on Pond Run Road was soaked with blood. People say a lot of things. Supposedly, a couple was once parked at the bridge and they were stabbed to death by some sort of pointy thing, probably resembling a hook.

Another version of the legend claims that a couple was parked at the bridge and heard a scratching sound coming from outside the car. Then, when the brave but careless boy got out of the car to investigate he was poked full of holes by the Hook Man!

Other versions of this legend involve a couple hearing that annoying scratching sound and then driving home only to find a hook sticking out of the roof of the car. Or the door. Or maybe the bumper. And it's bloody. And really scary. Sometimes the boyfriend gets killed and he's found on the top of the car. I find it incredible that this Hook Man keeps managing to find new hooks he can use for hands. He must have a vast collection of hook-hands back there in the woods somewhere.

If this is all sounding very familiar to you, it's because this popular legend has been featured in many movies and TV programs.

To make the legend even more incredulous, it is reported that sometime in the 1990s, groups of people were chased from the area by a van. Like so many other legends, there always seems to be a van to chase you away, just as things start to get interesting. Some were even chased away by a Greyhound bus. A GREYHOUND BUS? What? Who was on that bus and what was so scary about it? Couldn't you just pull over and let the bus drive by? If you are going to be scared to death by a Greyhound bus, you should just stay home. I don't understand this at all.

On January 21, 2009 I visited the site with documentary film maker and fellow researcher Andy Colvin. It was dusk when we got to the bridge to take a few photos and to take a look around. I can't say what others have experienced but I didn't notice anything particularly creepy or mysterious about the area, other than the fact that it is situated between some tall ridges and I'm sure it gets extra dark and spooky there at night. There were some men doing construction on top of a hill overlooking the bridge. Houses in the area don't seem particularly unusual to me.

We spent some time sitting at the bridge, taking photos and recording sound. Andy recorded some video while I walked up and down the road, waved my EMF meter around, and attempted to do some EVP recording with my digital voice recorder. We didn't pick up anything unusual in our video, photos, or audio recordings

"You hear that?"

"Hear what?"

"Dogs. Barking. For no reason."

The Woods Bordering Pond Run Road

While at the bridge, I did notice some dogs barking in the distance, but there's nothing mysterious about that. We have a dog next door who does the same thing. For "no apparent reason" - just like the dogs around Pond Run. Dogs like to bark. As for the mysterious sounds from the woods, I don't know how many times I have heard people reporting "strange" sounds coming from the woods. Is it because we spend too much time indoors and aren't familiar with the natural everyday sounds of nature?

I am sure the woods around this bridge are full of deer and other animals. I guess it's likely that they step on a tree branch now and then. Or maybe they will break off branches and tree bark in search of food like grubs and ants. Anyone who enjoys camping can tell you that the woods are full of sounds at night. I suppose that if you are the nervous type, you could imagine there is something in the woods coming to get you.

After our short investigation, we drove home. I looked into the rear-view mirror but didn't notice anyone trying to chase us away. No Greyhound bus with tinted windows.

According to some books and documentaries, people living near the bridge on Pond Run Road in New Richmond continue to hear strange sounds coming from the woods. The Hook Man legend is one of the most popular urban legends in the country. Even in the UK, there are numerous variations of the same Hook Man legend. Sometimes it's called the Murdered Boyfriend legend.

You probably know it because you've seen it in numerous horror movies and TV programs. A boy and girl are making out in the car and WHAM, the evil guy with a hook starts scratching around. Moments later, someone is stabbed by the Hook Man or they drive off with the hapless Hook Man's hand dangling from the car.

I haven't been able to dig up records to support any deaths from the Hook Man of Pond Run Road and I don't believe there is anything remotely paranormal about the area. Maybe I'm not looking carefully enough, or maybe I need to visit the area a few more times but it's really difficult for me to keep an open mind about this one. Maybe I would be convinced if I found a hook hanging from my car door but I believe the story is nothing more than that. Just a story.

DIRECTIONS: Pond Run Road is located off of US-52 in New Richmond, Ohio. The bridge is just up the road and passes over the creek (Pond Run itself).

Spooky Hollow Road

Spooky Hollow Road is located in Indian Hill, just a few miles northeast of the city of Cincinnati. First settled in 1795, the village of Indian Hill was called Camargo until it was officially incorporated in 1941. With a population of around 5,900, it is probably the most prosperous neighborhood in the Greater Cincinnati area. Many multi-million dollar estates populate the village as well as a few working farms and stables. Thickly wooded in many sections, its lavish gated homes typically sit at the end of very long driveways.

Several years ago, I was driving late one night when I decided to travel down Spooky Hollow Road. With tall trees bordering both sides, and no moonlight to illuminate the ground, it can be absolutely dark. When I was about halfway down the hollow, the headlights and all of the interior lights in my car suddenly went out and I found myself rolling down a very curvy 2-lane road in the middle of the night with no headlights!

I tried again and again to turn the car's headlights back on, without success. I stuck my head out of the window and strained to see the surface of the road but couldn't see any details. I don't suppose I was thinking rationally, but I felt that if I slammed the brakes, I would lose control of the car and roll into a ditch. For perhaps five to ten seconds I was in total darkness and then, just as suddenly as they had gone out, the headlights and interior lights came back on. I drove straight home. This was the first and only time I had experienced trouble with my car's electrical system.

The next day I told a friend at work about what had happened. He lived in the area and was very familiar with Spooky Hollow Road. He didn't seem at all surprised. "Yeah, that happens to a lot of people," he said. "That road is haunted."

If the road is really haunted, what could be the cause?

According to what I have learned from local residents and friends who have lived in Indian Hill, there is an old legend about the former Fleischmann Estate that borders Spooky Hollow Road. The legend says that the Fleischmann family had belonged to some sort of cult in France and when they moved to Indian Hill to build their new home, they used "albino demons" to protect the estate while they were away. When the last of the Fleischmann family moved out, the estate was left empty for several years and fell into ruin, leaving the demons to take control of the house and wander freely over the land.

It's difficult to tell how this legend started but the origins may lie somewhere in the history of the estate and the family who built it. In 1834, Charles L. Fleischmann was born in Jaegersdorf, a suburb of Vienna, Austria. He traveled briefly to America and married his wife Henriette in 1866 before moving to Hungary. Two years later he traveled back to America with his brother Max and a plan to start a new business. In 1868, Charles and Max, together with James Gaff, founded in Riverside, Ohio what became the first yeast manufacturing plant in America. In addition to yeast production, Charles was also responsible for several patents involving yeast production machinery. The Fleischmann Company eventually became the world's largest yeast producer (later becoming Standard Brands) and the second largest producer of vinegar. In addition, the Fleischmann name became America's first commercial producer of gin. It wasn't long before the family became world-class businessmen with yeast production plants all over America, dozens of yachts, valuable artwork, and the finest stable of racehorses in the country. Charles and his wife, Henriette, had three children – Julius, Maxmillian (who preferred to be called Max), and Bettie.

Born in Riverside, Ohio on February 26, 1877, Max C. Fleischmann, was an avid ballooner and during the First World War he was put in command of an American military ballooning school in Cuperly, France. In 1918 the school had to be abandoned because of German offenses, but Max continued to fly balloons when he got back to America, participating in many balloon demonstrations and competitions. An early Cincinnati postcard titled "Ascension of the Max Fleischmann Balloon" shows a balloon ready for launch with a crowd of curious onlookers standing below.

A Max Fleischmann Balloon In Cincinnati *

He was also an explorer, big game hunter, and an extremely well respected sportsman and conservationist. He donated much of his time and money to help establish the Nevada State

Museum in Carson City, as well as many worthwhile wildlife conservation projects. Furthermore, he was a 32nd degree Mason – a member of the Blue Lodge.

Max's brother Julius Fleischmann also grew up to be a leading philanthropist, outdoorsman, businessman, Mason, and politician, eventually taking over the family business. Among his many pursuits, Julius owned racehorses and yachts, was co-owner of the Cincinnati Baseball Club, a member of the Chamber of Commerce, president of several companies, and Mayor of Cincinnati from 1900 to 1905.

In 1924, Julius Fleischmann bought a 1,600-acre farm in Indian Hill and named it Winding Creek Farm. Designed by Stanley Matthews of Glendale and New York City, the main manor house was constructed of limestone taken from nearby Winding Creek and took about three years to complete. Being a passionate horseman, Fleischmann helped establish a local hunt club called the Camargo Hunt so that residents of this new community, now composed largely of wealthy city dwellers looking for fresh air and leisurely country living, could hunt foxes on their sprawling estates. A pack of foxhounds were donated to the club by Fleischmann and kept at his kennels on Spooky Hollow Road. He also built a cottage and stables for the huntsmen. Living in New York City at the time, Fleischmann must have eagerly looked forward to enjoying his beautiful new country manor home in Indian Hill.

On February 5, 1925, while away on one of his many trips, Julius was playing polo at the Nautilus Polo Field in Miami Beach, Florida when he suddenly collapsed and died of heart failure. Sadly, Julius Fleischmann never got a chance to see his new home at Winding Creek Farm.

After completion of the manor house and other buildings on the property in 1927, Winding Creek Farm became the home of Julius Fleischmann Junior and his wife Dorette who often used it to host social activities for family and friends. After Julius Fleischmann Junior died in 1968 and then his widow passed away in 1994, the estate began to feel the ravages of time. Over the years, the original 1,600-acre Winding Creek Farm was gradually divided up into smaller properties until it was reduced to just 343 acres in 1996. In 1998, Louis and Louise Nippert bought Winding Creek Farm and combined it with neighboring Greenacres Farm in order to create the Greenacres Foundation, a non-profit operating group dedicated to preserving Indian Hill's woodland and farmland as well as offering the public a variety of educational and recreational programs.

An Old Entrance To The Fleischmann Estate

Today, the original English Norman style Fleischmann manor with its moat, formal gardens, Tea House, and Chauffeur's Cottage, is part of the Greenacres South Estate and is used to host musical programs for adults and children, visual arts, drama, and dance. The Arts Center can also be reserved for private functions such as weddings and fundraisers. Surrounded once again by a lush landscape, the house has been restored to its former beauty. The renewed Riding Club Barn and stables have also become part of the Greenacres property.

So, now that the estate has been renovated and is being used for social functions and public education, what has happened to those albino demons once rumored to patrol the grounds? As far as I know, no one has come forth to report any demon activity, albino or otherwise. Even if they had once existed, does it make sense that demon guard dogs would be brought over from France? I wonder what the customs officials would have to say about it. In all probability, the stories of albino demons were made up by young people of Indian Hill who grew nervous when they saw the magnificent Fleischmann estate fall into a neglected state. Scary legends seem to grow around empty houses left unoccupied for any length of time. I have heard the same legend from many people and no one seems to know of a person who actually saw these creatures or experienced any kind of paranormal activity at the estate.

Demons or not, people still continue to report unexplained car trouble while driving on Spooky Hollow Road. I have traveled up and down the road many times and checked it for unusual electromagnetic activity – anything that would explain why a car's electrical system would fail and then just as mysteriously return to normal. I can't find a rational explanation for it. Maybe the ghosts of those old hunting dogs are galloping over the countryside, still chasing after foxes. Or cars.

Even if there are no paranormal shenanigans going on at the former Fleischmann Estate, there is something strange about the upper section of Spooky Hollow Road. If you believe in the sacred properties of the land, you may have your explanation for the unexplained activity.

Of course the community of Indian Hill did not always belong to the wealthy residents who live there today. When the first white settlers put down roots in the late 1700s, much of the area was occupied by the Shawnee people. According to local historians, Indian Hill got its name when settlers at what is now called Madisonville discovered that some Shawnee Indians had stolen a few of their horses. The settlers chased the Indians to the top of Indian Hill (which is now Indian Hill Road), where they caught up to one of the Indians, shot and killed him. Years later, his body was found on a farm above Madisonville, giving the name Indian Hill to the community.

Several prehistoric Native American mounds have been found around Indian Hill, which tells us that at least some of the land was used for religious ceremonies and burials. This land, now cleared to make homes and roads, may still be retaining some of its sacred properties. I can't say that this would be causing the kinds of paranormal activity experienced by people traveling on Spooky Hollow Road, but it is at least something to consider.

Old Photo Titled "*Exploiting the Graves of the Mound Builders near Madisonville*" Depicts The Desecration Of One Of The Mounds Found In Present-day Indian Hill *

In 1878, two mounds were discovered on present-day Drake Road. They were described as being circular, about three feet high and about four hundred feet in circumference. A cluster of mounds was found near where present-day Indian Hill Road leads down to Terrace Park and at least one other mound was found on Remington Road. Regrettably, these sacred mounds and other earthworks have since been destroyed.

It may surprise people to know that as late as 2006, the Shawnee people were still trying to regain ownership of their land in Ohio. In 2004, Terry Casey, a consultant to the Eastern Shawnee, had a plan to take back Indian Hill in order to build five to seven Native-owned gambling casinos. Indian Hill has remained relatively unchanged since 2004, so it seems that the tribe didn't get their land, but they may actually have a legal right to it. In 1794, When President Washington gave permission for John Cleves Symmes to buy the land as part of 330,000 acres called The Symmes Purchase, it may not have been a legal deal.

A federal law in 1790 said that only Congress could take land from the Indians, by ratified treaties. The Symmes Purchase was not a treaty and it was not ratified, which means that true ownership of the land is still open to legal debate. In addition, the survey performed for Symmes was a disaster - he surveyed land he had not paid for and sold land he did not own. After much confusion, the United States government eventually recognized the individual land purchases but the Symmes Purchase was so badly managed that it effectively killed any further large land sales by Congress.

DIRECTIONS: Spooky Hollow Road crosses Loveland-Madiera Road in Indian Hill, which is north of Cincinnati. The former Fleischmann Estate, now called the Greenacres Arts Center can be found at 8400 Blome Road, which intersects Spooky Hollow Road at the top of the hill. An administrative office is located at 8255 Spooky Hollow Road. All visits to sites on the property are by reservation only or as part of an organized program.

Lick Road

This dead-end road at the very edge of Hamilton County is said to be haunted by a woman who was killed some time ago. According to the legend, a 30-year old woman named Amy was murdered by her boyfriend and her body was discarded nearby.

When you turn onto Lick Road and travel for about a mile, the road ends at a locked metal gate. Beyond the gate lies Richardson Forest Preserve, a 265-acre conservation area maintained by the Hamilton County Park District.

People say that if you drive to the end of Lick Road, face your car towards the woods, and wait a while, the word "help" will appear on the surface of your car's window or windshield. Other people claim to hear strange sounds or screams coming from the woods. Beyond the gate, a dirt road leads about a hundred yards or so to a bridge over a deep gorge. It is believed that this may be the spot where Amy's body was dumped.

I first investigated this site on June 30, 2006. As I approached Lick Road, I dangled my EMF meter out the car window as I sometimes do when doing what I call a drive-by paranormal investigation, just to see if the meter would detect anything unusual. Sure enough, as I got to the intersection of Lick Road and Kemper Road, the EMF meter starting spiking wildly, telling me there was a very high level of electromagnetic activity in the area. It's not proof of anything, but many paranormal investigators believe that high levels of electromagnetic energy are a sign of possible paranormal activity. Supposedly, spirits can either utilize the electromagnetic energy in order to manifest or else the energy is a result of the spirit activity itself. Either way, an abnormal EMF reading is a good enough reason to stop the car to take a closer look.

Intersection Of Kemper Road and Lick Road

Just as you pull onto Lick Road, there is a place to the side where you can park your car. I parked here and got out to take more readings with my EMF meter. At first I thought I may have been picking up high EMF readings from the electrical lines overhead, but this wasn't the case. I pointed my meter at the lines and didn't get a reading at all. As I walked around the car, everything seemed normal. No unusual readings anywhere around the car or along the sides of the road. The only spot where I got unusual EMF readings was at the very intersection of the two roads. Again, I'm not saying this indicates anything paranormal, but it was something to make note of. Unusual EMF readings don't mean anything unless they change location or disappear. These readings seemed to stay consistent, leading me to believe there was some kind of natural source. Nothing paranormal here, unfortunately. Time to move on.

When I got back to the car, I started to walk around the outside of the car in order to take a series of digital photos. Right away the batteries in my camera went dead which is something that happens far too often when investigating haunted locations. After going back to the car for fresh batteries, I loaded new batteries into the camera and tried again. In two of the photos, I could see a very strange blurred outline. I would even go so far as to say the outline was shaped like a person. Again, this isn't proof of anything but photography was my major in college. I have even taught photography myself. I would say I have taken many thousands of photographs with all types of film and cameras, including digital, and I have never seen anything exactly like this. A human-shaped blur? I was standing outside the car at the time, so I am sure it wasn't a reflection from one of the car windows. The blur wasn't a smudge on the lens because I took several photos and the blurred outline only appeared on two of the photos. It wasn't raining or snowing and it wasn't foggy or humid. The sun didn't cause it because the same blur appeared on photos taken on opposite sides of the car, pointing in opposite directions. So what was it? Call it a photo glitch if you want, but it definitely sparked my curiosity.

Odd Human-Shaped Blur On The Side Of Lick Road

Wider View Of The Same Photo

Headless Brides and Devil Dogs

Another Gate At The Dead-End

Access to the area beyond the metal gate at the dead-end of Lick Road is firmly restricted by the park service but if you call them in advance, you can get permission to visit the area. After getting permission, I visited the site again and explored the area in the woods where "Amy's Bridge" is located. After you cross the metal gate, a dirt road leads to the left, around a bend to the bridge. I stood on the bridge alone for a while to try some EVP recording.

"Amy, are you here?"

"Is this the place where you died? Were you murdered?"

"Are you somewhere else? Is there anyone else here?"

"How did you die?"

I listened to the recordings later and didn't hear anything I would call EVP. I went back to the car to see if the word "help" had appeared on the inside of my windshield. No such luck. I stayed a while so I could try to get a feel for the surroundings. I don't think I am psychic or sensitive in the paranormal sense of the word, but this is something I do when investigating an allegedly haunted place. I sit quietly and listen. I try to tune into the surroundings, hoping some sort of psychic intuition will kick in. I sat. I stared at the woods. I waited. And after a while, I decided to pack up my gear and go home.

In early 2009 I returned to Lick Road with fellow paranormal researcher Andy Colvin. We parked at the dead-end and did some taping with our camcorders. I also tried again to record some EVP but I didn't pick up anything significant. I did a sweep with the EMF meter, just for good measure. While Andy waited in the car, I walked back to the bridge to try some more recording and to take a few photos. Eventually we gave up and left the area empty handed.

Was there ever really a woman named Amy? Was she murdered here? Is this area haunted? As it is with most of these legends passed down from person to person over the years, we really don't have any solid information to go on. No one cares about the details as long as it's a good story. Even if someone died here, can anyone tell me where she was murdered or where the body was found? Is there a police report? Having some verifiable information like this would make it easier to find a ghost, if it actually exists. If the story of Amy is true, who's to say her body wasn't dumped at the opposite end of Lick Road, at the place where it intersects Kemper? That's where I got the abnormal EMF readings and it's where I got the unusual photos. Are people parking at the dead-end simply because it looks creepier down there?

Numerous people today are naturally afraid of thickly wooded areas. I think it has something to do with our heritage. When European settlers first came to America, they feared the woods for good reason. The woods were full of danger. Even today, when the city streets of our country are far more dangerous than anything found in nature, many people still have a deep-seated, primal fear of the woods, especially if we are not used to being outdoors. And this fear grows stronger at night.

Although there are people who have reported hearing unexplainable sounds coming from these woods, the sounds are probably not paranormal in nature.

Richardson Forest Preserve, the woods at the end of Lick Road, is a conservation area filled with wildlife. The area is used for hiking, bird watching, and hunting. The deer population in the reserve is overpopulated now to a level where the park service allows controlled bow hunting from September to February. Deer and many other animals are nocturnal. That is, they come out at night. Anyone parked at the edge of the preserve, expecting to hear "strange" sounds coming from the woods, is likely to hear the normal sounds of deer, raccoons, possums, and other animals. These sounds would seem spooky and unusual only if you were unfamiliar with common sounds of the woods at night. A bewildering sound coming from the bridge could easily be the sound of a deer or other animal foraging in the woods or going to the creek at the bottom of the gorge to get a drink of water.

Or it could be ordinary living people.

Kids come to this road all the time to see if they can experience something scary. They take their friends and have a good time trying to convince each other that there is a ghost outside their car, scratching at the trunk or creeping around in the dark. Some of the kids will tell you they were chased from the area by some kind of van or truck. This is the same thing you hear about many of the allegedly haunted places in southern Ohio. There's always a van to chase you away. Sometimes it's white. Sometimes it's black.

If anyone is trying to chase people from Lick Road, it is probably the people who have to live there and put up with the nightly parade of people looking for ghosts. If we assume for a minute that there is a ghost here and that she is writing the word "help" on everyone's car window, why hasn't anyone tried to help her?

If you do visit the site and you believe the stories, at least wish her well. Say a prayer or something. If you think you have mediumistic abilities, maybe you could come here to see if this Amy person actually needs help crossing over. It's just a thought. Maybe someday we will find out who killed her and why, provided the story is true. If we can do that, maybe Amy will be able to rest in peace.

DIRECTIONS: Lick Road is located east of U.S 27 (Colerain Avenue), just off of Kemper Road in Colerain Township. Since the end of the road is very dark and isolated, there is a chance you may run into someone dangerous or unfriendly. I would **not** advise going there after dark. Never trespass. If you do visit and want to explore the woods beyond the gate (notice the sign that says RESTRICTED AREA – NO TRESPASSING), call the Hamilton County Park Service to get permission. Many people do use the area for hiking and hunting, but you must get permission first. Just call the park rangers and ask. Be particularly careful during bow hunting season.

The Screaming Bridge of Maud Hughes Road

Every state seems to have a few "Crybaby Bridge" stories. They usually involve a woman throwing a baby from the bridge, committing suicide at the bridge, or some other horrific act. Our local version of the legend would be the Screaming Bridge of Maud Hughes Road in Liberty Township, Ohio.

The simple bridge passes about 25 feet over railroad tracks which became part of the New York Central Freight rail line at the beginning of the 1900s. According to newspaper reports, on Sunday morning October 24, 1909, a freight train was heading north along these tracks when the train's steam boiler blew, scalding two engineers to death. It is said that the ghosts of the two engineers can still be seen walking the line between the Screaming Bridge and Gano, Ohio to the north.

In addition to ghostly hooded figures seen around the bridge, people claim to see odd glowing red lights, foggy shapes, and sometimes even a complete phantom train.

A newspaper article from the Indiana Evening Gazette, Indiana, PA 25 Oct 1909 describes the accident:

Gano, Ohio Train Wreck
October 25, 1909
CARS PILE UP IN WRECK
Two Killed and Three Injured in Accident on Big Four.

Cincinnati, Oct. 25.-Two men were killed and three others seriously injured when an engine of a freight train exploded while running at full speed on the Big Four railroad near Gano station, twenty-five miles north of here. Six cars of the train piled on top of the wrecked engine and several thousand dollars' worth of freight was destroyed in the fire that followed. The entire train was derailed. The dead are: OSCAR PRICE, engineer, Springfield, O.; CHARLES WYCOFF, engineer, Middletown, O. The injured are: HARRY GOBB, head brakeman, Reading, O.; CLAUDE MOCH, fireman, Springfield, O.; HARRY JONES, conductor, Cincinnati. Both engineers who were killed were married and had families.

The train's tender had been loaded with plenty of water before it left Ivorydale in Cincinnati. Unknown to the crew, after a run of only about 11 to 12 miles, a leak had drained much of the water, causing the steam engine to overheat and explode. One of the victims, engineer Charles Wycoff, had been off duty and was hitching a ride back to his home in Middletown. The steam locomotive exploded while traveling at about 40 miles per hour.

On June 7, 1976, another horrible accident occurred on the same section of rail line, not far from the accident of 1909. At the tracks beneath the Princeton Road overpass in Liberty Township, a Penn Central employee was killed when two rails protruding from a southbound work train penetrated the cab of a northbound Penn Central diesel locomotive.

So it seems there were at least three deaths on the railroad tracks running near the so-called Screaming Bridge of Maud Hughes Road but railroad workers aren't the only ones believed to be haunting the area. There are also reports that sometime during the 1970s some boys were struck and killed by a train farther south where the train tracks intersect Hamilton Mason Road.

These are true events associated with train accidents in the vicinity and many people believe that sudden violent deaths can be the cause of haunting activity - but there are other legends that have grown over the years. These legends are more associated with the bridge itself.

One legend tells of a man and woman who were driving one night when their car broke down on this bridge. The story claims that the couple had a fight and the woman either fell or was pushed from the bridge onto the tracks below. Another variation claims that the man left the woman in the car while he went to get help. When he returned to the car, he found the woman hanging from the bridge. The man also died, though the legend doesn't say how this happened. Supposedly on certain nights you are still able to hear their conversation or the sounds of a man's scream followed by a woman's scream - hence the name, Screaming Bridge.

Another story follows the more typical "Crybaby Bridge" urban legend format - the woman throws her baby from the bridge and then hangs herself from the bridge. I have found no evidence to support any of these stories, but they are a good example of how urban legends can change over the years, becoming more elaborate or taking on details from other legends.

It would be interesting to do some research to see if you could find any newspaper articles or police reports regarding accidents and suicides at the Screaming Bridge. I have found none and yet some people claim that there have been many deaths here. People continue to come to the bridge to see if they can hear the ghostly screams or perhaps see an apparition. I think that if they are actually witnessing paranormal phenomena of any kind, the phenomena are more connected to railroad accidents than to the Screaming Bridge. It's my belief that the legends about the bridge have been made up by people seeing or hearing something unusual and then trying to enhance their stories to make them more entertaining.

Or of course there could be nothing paranormal here at all.

Or I could be totally wrong and there could be ghosts all over the place!

I guess the only way to find out is to forget the legends and to investigate the Screaming Bridge for yourself. With an open mind and a healthy dose of skepticism, if at all possible.

I first investigated the road on June 16, 2007. As I approached the bridge to take some photos, my camera batteries died, which made me have to walk back to the car for fresh batteries. A raccoon waddled across the bridge and I could hear a train passing below me as I took photos. While I was on the bridge, I attempted to record some EVP but I didn't get anything unusual. I didn't see any hooded apparitions or hear any screams. Like all allegedly haunted locations, a lot of patience is needed. You can't really expect instant gratification, even if the place is haunted. One person who claims to be psychic told me he once saw the apparition of a young girl here. If so, it would be interesting to find out her identity and how she came to be at the bridge.

Of course there could be some natural non-paranormal explanations for unexpected sights and sounds in the area. Someone who grew up in a house less than 200 feet from the Screaming Bridge told me that the crying or screaming sounds people have heard at the overpass are probably the sounds of an Eastern Screech Owl she knows to have lived in the woods there. If you were parked at the bridge late at night and expecting to hear something spooky, it would be easy to mistake the Screech Owl's call for a human scream.

Strange sounds are one thing, but what about apparitions and strange lights reported in the area? Could there be a natural explanation for these? Train tracks are known to emit strong infrasound, extremely low frequencies of sound that could account for some of the strange feelings and impressions people get while investigating the area. Infrasound is sound with a very low frequency, below the range of human hearing. It can cause some very weird sensations such as physical pressure, fear, disorientation, or negative physical and mental symptoms.

There is also the possibility of high electromagnetic emissions in the area that may account for some of the odd lights or glows, although I couldn't detect anything abnormal when I visited the bridge. Sometimes, people at haunted locations will report that they feel sick or uncomfortable when exposed to strong electromagnetic fields (EMF). They may feel dizzy or they may feel that the location is giving them an uneasy feeling. Unusually high levels of electromagnetic energy can cause all of these sensations, or even hallucinations, especially if you are hypersensitive to electromagnetic radiation, as many people are.

I find it fascinating that some people have reported seeing glowing red lights bobbing along the tracks because I used to own an old kerosene railroad lantern with a red globe. These red lanterns, called Brakemen's Lamps or Danger Lamps, were carried by the train's brakemen and used to signal dangers such as a decoupling in the train, a blockade, sudden stop, or other emergency. Certainly an exploding steam engine or impact with another train would be a good reason to start waving a red lantern. Are people really seeing the ghosts of railroad workers wandering up and down the tracks? Are the phantom workmen still waving their Danger Lamps?

Seemingly paranormal railroad lamps have been seen in many other locations such as the famous Maco Ghost Light of Maco, North Carolina. According to this famous legend, the light is caused by a railroad lamp carried by a deceased train conductor named Joe Baldwin. Supposedly, in 1867 Joe was aboard his train and heading home to Wilmington when he started to walk from the last coach of the train to announce that the train was nearing its destination. When he opened the front door of the coach, he was horrified to see that the rest of the train had decoupled and was far ahead of him. To make matters worse, his coach car was slowing down and another train was coming up close behind at high speed. Joe tried until the very end to use his railroad lamp to warn the train coming up from behind, but it was too late. The approaching train slammed into Joe's coach car, decapitating him.

According to this legend, you can still see Joe's lantern swinging back and forth as Joe searches for his missing head on the stretch of railroad track where the accident took place. So many people have seen the light that, allegedly, the railroad has ordered its signalmen at Maco to use two signal lights, one red and one green, to avoid another accident.

There are actually two or three different locations involved in the legend of the Screaming Bridge of Maud Hughes Road. The first train accident attributed to the Screaming Bridge happened in West Chester Township, some distance away from the Screaming Bridge, which is located in Liberty Township. Are people going to the wrong location? It would be interesting to investigate the site of the second train accident near the Princeton Road bridge. I don't think people are aware of this second location, which could be haunted. The bridge over Princeton Road may even be the source of some of the old stories and ghost sightings. Could people be confusing one overpass for another?

And here's something to think about – if the legends are more than just legends, could there be multiple hauntings in the area?

DIRECTIONS: The bridge is located at a point north of where Maud Hughes Road crosses Princeton Road in Liberty Township. When Maud Hughes meets Princeton, it does a short bypass and is picked up several yards up Princeton Road.

Screaming Bridge is situated on two sharp curves in the road that go over a double set of railroad tracks. There are several bridges in the same area, so be sure you have the right one. Screaming Bridge is about a half mile north of where it meets Princeton Road.

There is a highway patrol station just down the road. Traffic is busy here during the day, so be careful if you visit the bridge.

There is a place to park about 200 yards past the bridge but there isn't much room for walking. Visibility on the bridge is poor at night so be extremely cautious.

The Highway To Heaven

Because of the unusually high number of fatal automobile accidents on this stretch of highway in Ohio, the section of U.S. 27 between the northern boundary of Colerain Township (near northern Cincinnati) and Oxford has been nicknamed the Highway To Heaven. In the year 2000 alone, there were 10,070 accidents involving teens in the county, causing 17 deaths.

At one time, actual road signs that read "Highway To Heaven" used to mark this section of highway, but they have since been removed. Maybe they were bad for business. Maybe they were too grim a reminder of the many deaths which have occurred and continue to occur here.

Many of the crosses have been removed too. Crosses marking the spots where people have lost their lives. The road is dangerous for many reasons. The 2-lane highway curves through rolling farmland and is marked with a variety of posted speed limits. Many parts of the road have no shoulders and in spots it is flanked by deep ravines on both sides. People always seem to be in a hurry to get to the college town of Oxford or back towards Cincinnati, Fairfield, or Hamilton.

I had my own close encounter with death on this road several years ago when I was driving home late one night. I was driving south at about 50 miles per hour. At a point just south of Millville, I suddenly fell asleep at the wheel. My car rocketed off the road, over a deep ravine, and straight into a large tree. The car was totally demolished. Somehow I managed to get out of the car but the rest of the night is a blur.

I remember walking around and around the car, in shock, not knowing if I was alive or dead. I can understand now how people can report that ghosts haunt certain locations because they have died suddenly and spend eternity wandering around in a state of confusion, not even aware that they are dead. I think I would have been one of these poor confused souls if I had died that night.

My Car After The Accident

Even though the doors of my car were still closed when they towed it to the scrap yard the next day, I can't remember getting out of the car. I was alone and both doors were crushed, so I am not even sure if I could have opened them.

Just before I crashed, I remember my face smashing into the steering wheel. The force was enough to break the steering wheel in half. I could hear tires screeching, then a rumbling sound as my car left the road, and then a sudden CRUNCH. I was knocked unconscious for a while. When I awoke the first time, I was in complete darkness and I can remember feeling blood on my face and on my leg. "I guess I'm dead," I thought, and then I blacked out again.

The second time I awoke, I was standing in a field outside my car, looking at the car and walking around and around it. Then I blacked out again.

When I awoke for the third time, I was sitting in someone's car and I can remember they had a small First Aid kit. They were trying to render aid and I can remember telling them I was sorry to be bleeding all over the front seat of their car.

When I awoke for the fourth time, I was being loaded into the back of an ambulance. My recollection of the night is very fuzzy, but my sister tells me she heard that as I was loaded into the ambulance, I asked the EMTs to thank the man who had stopped to help me. According to my sister, they told me there was no man. I was the only person on the scene. There had never been anyone there but me. To this day, my sister believes I was saved by a guardian angel. I have no idea what happened, but I am thankful to anyone, human or angelic, who may have stopped to help me that night.

Other people who have crashed near here have not been as lucky as I was. Three men died in an accident at almost the same spot - just south of Millville on March 30, 2002.

I personally know a few other people who have had accidents on this part of U.S. 27. A couple of friends once lost control of their car and rolled it over several times before coming to rest, upside down, on the side of the road. Another close call on this deadly highway.

Parking Lot Of The Shady-Nook Restaurant

About halfway between Oxford and Millville is the old Shady-Nook restaurant. Once a busy spot on U.S. 27, it is closed now but in front of the restaurant is one of the Highway To Heaven's most dangerous curves. A young man named Rick was killed in an accident here in 1971.

A man named Gerald (Jerry) was killed on the Highway To Heaven in December 20, 2003. A cross marks the place where he died after being struck head-on by another vehicle near Kirchling Road.

I think if roads can indeed be haunted, U.S. 27 between Cincinnati and Oxford should be one of the most haunted roads in America. There is something about it that causes drivers to become careless and sleepy, especially late at night. Though dotted with rural houses, the road has a desolate and lonely feel to it. During the day, drivers become impatient and often try to pass trucks, tractors, or slower cars. This has been the cause of many of the fatalities. Simple impatience.

Crosses At Kemper Road Exit

The section of highway just north of Ross is particularly dangerous, possibly because northbound motorists are anxious to break free from the bumper-to-bumper traffic. Traffic starts to thin out at this section of the road where it leaves the suburbs and becomes more of a standard highway. Cars anxiously accelerate to 70 - 80 miles per hour once they pass Struble Road. Further north, just past Rumpke Dump on the right, is the exit to Kemper Road. I've had my own close calls at this exit because there is little warning and cars behind you don't have a lot of time to react if you suddenly slow down to take the exit. A roadside cross marks the spot where a young girl named Steph died here in 2005. Several more crosses dot the area. Just last night, there was another accident on this road, near Stahlheber Road, sending two people to the hospital. One had to be transported by helicopter.

There are no particular legends attached to the Highway To Heaven. No ghost sightings that I know of. I have driven over this section of highway hundreds of times and I have never seen anything out of the ordinary.

Heading North, Near Kirchling Road

I include it in this book only because this is one of southern Ohio's mysterious places. It could be simple human carelessness causing all of the accidents on this part of the highway, or it could be something else. For now, I don't have reason to believe there is anything paranormal about it, but I become very nervous whenever I am on this section of U.S. 27. If nothing else, it is a good idea to be extra cautious when driving on the Highway To Heaven.

DIRECTIONS: The Highway To Heaven is a nickname given to the section of U.S. 27 (Colerain Avenue), just north of Cincinnati, beginning generally where it intersects Struble Road and ending at Oxford, Ohio.

The Headless Ghost of Dunlap

The village of Dunlap (originally called Georgetown) was one of the earliest villages to emerge in Colerain Township. It was first laid out on September 2, 1829 at the junction of Colerain Pike and Kemper Road. The George Struble farm lay just east of Colerain Pike and the new village may have been named after him. It picked up the new name of Dunlap when John Dunlap's post office was moved here from the old Cotton Mill in Colerain Village, a couple of miles down the hill where Toad Creek meets the Great Miami River.

The new post office was established in 1837, with David Wallace as Postmaster, and the small town of Dunlap began to grow.

"The village on the hill" soon had a blacksmith shop, hotel, stores, taverns, and enough to keep the local farmers busy. The people of Dunlap always looked forward to the mail coach making its four-hour run from Cincinnati. Farmers on the outskirts of Dunlap would come into town to catch up on gossip, have a couple of drinks, and learn what was happening in the big city of Cincinnati.

On the afternoon of September 9, 1887, it is believed that a small boy playing with matches may have started a fire. In spite of some heroic efforts by Ralph Struble, who climbed onto a roof to throw water onto the Hornung's store, and Sam Brook who was able to save George Klemm's buildings, the fire quickly spread throughout the town.

In those days, there was no fire department in Dunlap. If a fire broke out, they would have had to use buckets of water, carried by hand, to quench the flames. Residents depended on water drawn from wells or pumps. It is said that a single bucket of water would have been enough to put out this fire if it had been caught in time but there were no wells close at hand and the only nearby water pump was locked.

Lost that day were houses, stables, a saloon, a blacksmith shop, a store, a set of hay scales, and several outbuildings. A total of eleven buildings were burned to ashes. The families of Dan Diefenbacher, Asher Pickens, and Amos Pickens lost their homes and nearly all of their belongings. It was a devastating day for the village on the hill.

Of course this tragedy was big news to neighboring communities. Newspaper reporter Robert Mulford was sent from the nearby village of Venice to cover the event for his employer, The Venice Graphic. As he began to ask questions, he recalled a strange story he had published in the paper that very day. While vacationing at his friend George Richard's home just a week before the fire, he had heard about a headless man who once appeared nightly on the streets of Dunlap! This ghoulish figure was said to be the ghost of a man who had been murdered sometime in the town's early days.

According to the legend recorded by Robert Mulford, a man named Stimson had claimed a section of land and began clearing it for farming. After clearing the land, he erected a log cabin and dug a well. All seemed fine to Mr. Stimson until another man, perhaps a wealthier or more influential man, claimed that Stimson's claim overlapped his own. A land dispute erupted between the two men and Stimson was forced to move, leaving his home and land behind. Angry over the loss of all that he owned, it is said that Stimson murdered the other man and threw his headless body down the well.

I myself have not been able to find the place where Stimson lived, but this is the legend, as recorded by Mulford, and for a long time after the murder it is said that his ghost roamed nightly throughout the village. Children would not go anywhere near the abandoned well after dark.

By the time Robert Mulford recorded the story for the Venice Graphic in 1887, the well was filled with dirt and debris. Little was left of Stimson's property except for a bare outline where the cabin once stood. The well was just a depression in the ground, barely visible. Today, this physical evidence is surely long gone. The name of the man Stimson was suspected of murdering was never recorded and I can find no records of a Stimson staying to live in Dunlap. Perhaps he moved on to stake another claim elsewhere.

But what about the fire many years later? It seems ironic to me that the fire could have been extinguished if the townspeople had been able to access just one more source of water. I am not sure where it was located but if it had survived, Stimson's well may have made all the difference to the people of Dunlap. It's a shame too that a watering trough just outside of town, built by Giles Richards in 1867, could have provided water to extinguish the fire. Unfortunately, it was too far away to be useful.

Maybe the fire was a cruel curse put upon the town by the murdered man or by Stimson who was forced to give up everything he had worked for. Maybe the little boy had nothing to do with the fire. I guess we will never know.

Watering Trough On Old Colerain, Built In 1867

There is no proof that there was ever a headless ghost wandering around in Dunlap, but the story is generally regarded as true. In 1954 the village finally got its own fire department, in case anyone else decides to play with matches. In 1975, the Groesbeck and Dunlap fire departments merged, forming the Colerain Township Fire Department.

I have made no attempts to authenticate this haunting but I present it here as an interesting piece of folklore. After all of these years, it would be impossible to interview witnesses to the ghost sightings. As far as I know, no one has seen the famous ghost since the days shortly after the fire of 1887.

DIRECTIONS: Dunlap, Ohio is located on Old Colerain, off of U.S. 27 (Colerain Avenue) in Colerain Township. The main part of Dunlap is located where West Kemper Road meets Old Colerain.

Buell Road

Like so many of the rural and suburban roads in Colerain Township, Buell Road is hilly, curved, and filled with hidden dangers. Following the road from where it connects to Pippin Road, it passes Triple Creek Park and takes a couple of sharp turns before reaching the only straight section of the road.

It is here, along the straight part of the road, where legend says that you can see the ghost of a small boy on a bicycle. Supposedly, if you park your car on this part of the road at night, flash your car's headlights three times, and wait a while, you will hear the squeaky sounds of the boy's bicycle come up from behind you. Some say that you can even see him as he gets nearer and nearer. Just before he reaches you, he will disappear. Another version of the legend claims that if the ghost bicycle manages to reach your car, you will die… in seven days.

This legend has been around for a long time and seems to be a concoction of common legends heard all over the country. Tales of ghost bicycles, ghost motorcycles, and ghost cars abound. They are entrenched into the consciousness of young people everywhere, and the inspiration for these imaginative stories is undoubtedly kept alive by hundreds of horror movies. Take a few bored teenagers, throw in a spooky legend, and you have something to do on weekends. Who can say how many people have waited by the side of the road to listen for this squeaky bicycle? How many have looked nervously over their shoulders, expecting a ghostly boy to materialize out of the darkness?

No matter how many times people come here, they never really see this ghost bicycle and as far as I know, the story is a complete fabrication. No bicycle accident. No ghost. It is just another one of those legends that never seems to go away.

However, Buell Road has recently seen real tragedy. On May 29, 2007, three carloads of kids were following each other home from school. After leaving nearby Northwest High School onto Pippin Road, they turned right onto Buell Road. The cars navigated a few curves and then sped up as they reached the straight part of the road. It was a hot day. Partly sunny and eighty eight degrees. The road was dry. According to the Hamilton County police report publicly released after the accident, this is what happened:

In the lead car were Peter Tyler, Allison Keller, and Andrew Peter. Allison Keller told the police, "We went around the first couple corners, just like we normally did, and everything was fine. As we were pretty far down the straight away Tyler started screaming saying we need to go back there, we need to go back there. When he started screaming I looked back and just saw trees and branches falling."

The middle car, driven by an inexperienced 16-year old Chad Metzcar, was carrying four other passengers. In the car with him were Lauren Dietz, Miranda Phelps, Dustin Listerman, and Derrick Listerman. According to estimates by the police, Metzcar was driving at least 70 miles per hour when the posted speed limit on that road is only 35 miles per hour.

Peter Tyler, driver of the lead car, heard a squealing sound behind him. When he looked into his rear view mirror, he could see Metzcar's car lose control and veer off into the trees. Tree branches and leaves were falling all around. As the kids got out of their cars to call 911 and run to the aid of their friends, they could hear the screams.

A few witnesses also stopped their cars to see if they could assist but for 14-year old Lauren Dietz and 15-year old Miranda Phelps, it was too late. Both girls died at the scene. The other passengers in the car were taken to the hospital for treatment.

Investigators admitted the obvious - speed contributed to the girls' deaths. That and the fact that the three people in the back seat of Metzcar's car, including the two girls who died, were not wearing seat belts. Like so many automobile accidents, this one could have been avoided by simply slowing down. I have driven on this road many times and I think that 35 miles per hour is about as fast as you can safely travel over this road, even if it does have one deadly straight section.

Roadside Memorial

On the site of the accident, people have erected a roadside memorial to honor the memory of Lauren Dietz and Miranda Phelps. A gloomy collection of crosses, ribbons, and hand-made signs. I visited the site during a snowstorm on January 7, 2009 just to take a few photos. Skid marks still scarred the road. Someone has left a hammer, so people can pound the crosses into the ground when they fall. I tried to fix one of these fallen crosses but the ground was too frozen.

I do not believe the ghost bicycle is worth a serious investigation and I only mention it here to document it as one of our area's persistent folk legends. I have visited the site several times, day and night, and I have seen no sign of a ghost on a bicycle. I even flashed my headlights a few times. Nothing unusual was observed. Only a sad piece of road and a memorial reminding us to drive safely.

DIRECTIONS: Buell Road intersects Pippin Road just south of Northwest High School in Colerain Township. If you visit the memorial, please be careful. There are really no safe places to park a car. If you must visit the site, either keep moving or else find somewhere else to park. Never get out of the car after dark. In spite of this terrible accident, people continue to drive recklessly on Buell Road.

Princeton Road

Many towns have their phantom hitchhikers. This seems to be one of the most persistent of all urban myths. The story always goes something like this: Someone driving at night will pick up a hitchhiker, drop them off at their destination, and then find out later that the person they picked up had died years ago.

Our own local version of the story involves a woman who was also killed in an automobile accident. Supposedly, our local lady died on Princeton Road, just east of Hamilton, Ohio. She can sometimes be seen at the side of the road, warning drivers of danger up ahead. Sometimes, she is said to hitch a ride with someone if they are kind enough to stop for her.

The alleged sightings are said to appear along Princeton Road near Rose Hill Burial Park. Some people say they have seen her crossing the road and entering the cemetery. Perhaps, if this ghost really exists, this is where the woman is buried. Or maybe it just happens that her automobile accident occurred nearby. Is she still trying to find her way home? If she is warning people of some danger on Princeton Road, what kind of danger is she trying to tell us about? Is she pointing to the place where she died?

Entrance To Rose Hill Burial Park

Most of these phantom hitchhiker stories seem to be variations on one of the most famous ghost stories of all time, Resurrection Mary. The Resurrection Mary legend begins in 1934 when a young girl is killed in an auto accident while on her way home from the O. Henry Ballroom on Archer Avenue in Justice, Illinois, a suburb of Chicago. Five years later, in 1939, a cab driver picks up a young girl in a white gown on Archer Avenue. She sits beside him on the front seat and instructs him to drive north on Archer. After driving a short distance, she suddenly tells him to stop in front of Resurrection Cemetery and then she simply vanishes. Of course Resurrection Cemetery is where the girl, who had died five years earlier, is buried.

You can find similar legends from all around the country. Another variation has a boy giving a girl a ride home. She has them stop somewhere before they reach the house and since it is raining, the boy lends the girl his coat and tells her he will be back later to pick it up. The next day he drives to the girl's house and attempts to retrieve the coat but the woman who answers the door tells him their daughter, who he describes to her, had died several years ago on that very road. The boy goes to visit the girl's grave and his coat is there, covering the grave. Why the boy didn't just take the girl to her front door instead of dropping her off in the rain is probably a bigger mystery, but that's the way it goes with these urban legends. They don't have to make a lot of sense as long as the story is creepy enough. Mix the details around a little and you have a concoction of legends heard everywhere. The "Vanishing Hitchhiker" legend is a popular one.

At any rate, our ghostly woman should have no trouble finding a ride, since Princeton Road is a busy place. That's the problem we face when trying to investigate any of these old legends. The area where the event is supposed to have occurred is so completely different or obliterated by new construction, it is impossible to do a real paranormal investigation. Even when we know the exact details, the landscape has changed over the years. The area may have once been a spooky country road but over time it has transformed into a row of strip malls and car lots, with so much traffic going back and forth, it is impossible to take photographs or to do recordings. Light, noise, and electrical fields in the area will contaminate your evidence if you are lucky enough to get any.

I have found no evidence to support the idea that there is a ghost haunting the side of Princeton Road near the Rose Hill Burial Park, but does that mean she doesn't exist? No, of course not.

"I don't believe in ghosts because I have never seen one." This is what most people will tell you, but have they ever really looked? Are they out there, actively searching for ghosts? It's easy to be an armchair skeptic, waiting for other people to bring you proof of life after death. Are the stories in this book difficult to believe? Sure. Preposterous? Absolutely. I think it is up to each of us to examine the legends, search for the truth, and to come to our own conclusions. Behind every legend lies the possibility of a real paranormal event.

Inside Rose Hill Burial Park

Princeton Road – If There Was A Ghost Here, Would You Even Know?

DIRECTIONS: Rose Hill Burial Park is located at 2421 Princeton Road in Hamilton, Ohio.

Afterword

When I first set out to write a book about haunted roads and bridges, I didn't realize what a dangerous project it would be. I was alone most of the time and I visited some very isolated places. Some were country roads where visibility was poor, even in the daytime. Others were busy city streets where I had to be very careful not to get struck by traffic.

I encountered roads with no shoulders, which meant there was no safe place to walk or park my car. One or two of the sites were in high-crime areas. The day after I first investigated Rapid Run Park, there was an attempted kidnapping at the park. Ghost hunting can be very dangerous, for a lot of reasons. Forget the ghosts – it's the LIVING people you have to watch out for.

In August 2006, a 17-year old girl in Worthington, Ohio was shot in the head while ghost hunting with her friends. According to the newspaper report, the girls stepped onto a man's property to investigate the house because they had heard that the house was "spooky" and haunted. When they approached the house, the man living inside became scared and fired some shots out of his bedroom window to scare the trespassers away. The girls jumped back into their car and drove around the block. After they circled the block and drove past the man's house again, they heard a second round of shots. One of the girls was struck by gunshots to her head and shoulder, and then taken to the hospital where she arrived in critical condition.

If you decide to personally visit any of the locations in this book, please be very careful! Never trespass onto private property without permission and without giving advance notice. Contrary to what some people think, it doesn't matter whether the property is marked with signs or not. It is still against the law to go onto private property without the owner's consent. Public parks are generally open to everyone but only during operating hours. Some places like the Richardson Forest Preserve require that you check in with the Park Service first to get permission. This is especially important during hunting season.

Some sections of otherwise public areas may have restricted access. If in doubt, always check first. It's not difficult to do. Just look up the telephone number and give them a call. Never assume you can wander freely. Unfortunately, some areas have restricted access for very good reasons. Always watch your back and be careful not to go to isolated areas where there may be drug or gang activity. Even though I have investigated many places alone, I strongly recommend that you go only with a group. Sadly, it just isn't safe to go anywhere alone these days, plus if you were to fall or get injured, it is always best to have someone there to help you.

Because so many of these locations are on dangerous curves, narrow bridges, or roads without shoulders, be extra careful if you visit any of these places at night. The biggest danger is that you may be hit by another car or truck. Remember to use good common sense and always obey the law.

Glossary

WPA - Work Progress Administration (WPA) was a public works program developed by Franklin D. Roosevelt in the 1930s. The WPA provided income to the unemployed during the Great Depression by creating jobs such as road and bridge construction. One such project was the development of Rapid Run Park in Cincinnati.

Sensitive - A Sensitive, in the paranormal sense of the word, is a person who has a degree of psychic abilities. Sensitives have intuitive skills which help them to make contact with the non-physical world in many different ways. Sometimes they simply pick up on the "vibe" of a location and can emotionally tune into the location's history, including the emotions of people who have been there previously. Sometimes they are able to hear, see, or smell things which are not really part of the physical world, allowing them to sense their surroundings in a more enhanced way than most people. If a Sensitive is too open to this type of emotional stimulation, they can become anxious or overwhelmed.

Native American / Indian - In this book, I may use the words "Indian" and "Native American" interchangeably. I don't mean any disrespect. I know that some people prefer one term over the other. I would rather refer to people by their tribe. For example, I would not usually call a Shawnee Indian an Indian or a Native American. I would call them a Shawnee. Being part Native American myself (Shawnee), I am never sure which way is more correct. Some Native people will tell you that anyone born in America is a Native American.

EMF - (which stands for "Electromagnetic Field") is a field of energy created by electrically charged objects. An electromagnetic field has two "components", a magnetic component and an electric component. The electric field is produced by stationary charges, and the magnetic field by moving charges (currents). Electromagnetic fields are also often referred to as "Electromagnetic Radiation" (EMR). You can't see, feel or hear electromagnetic fields, apart from visible light, which is a part of the electromagnetic spectrum. It is believed that ghosts are made up of a type of energy or that it may be possible that they somehow use energy in order to materialize or to affect the environment, so when we search for unusual EMF readings we are actually searching for the possible presence of ghosts. But first, we must try to rule out all man-made sources of electromagnetic energy. Investigators use tools called EMF meters to search for sources of electromagnetic energy. Generally, if a strong electromagnetic field is detected and it stays consistent, never moving, then it is probably a man-made or natural field. However, if you detect an EMF reading that seems to fluctuate (change) wildly or change position, you may be detecting something paranormal. This is why paranormal investigators use EMF meters to search for ghosts.

EVP - It is believed by many that the voices and sounds of people who have passed into the spirit world can be recorded with ordinary recording devices. We call these sounds Electronic Voice Phenomena (EVP). It is not really known how this works but it does and it is something that many people do at allegedly haunted locations. The technique is very simple and you don't need any special hardware or computer software. Anything that can record sound can be used. You simply record at the location and listen to the recording later, preferably through headphones. Sometimes spirit voices will be heard inbetween or over top of your own conversations. A preferred technique is to ask a question, wait a while, and then to ask another question, much like you would do if you were interviewing a living person. Then you take the recording home and listen to it later.

Kokopelli Katsina - The buildings of Tiny Town were covered with what may or may not have been random Native American symbolism. One of the characters depicted was the Kokopelli Katsina, an ancient humpbacked flute player icon seen in artwork and crafts made by the Hopi and other southwestern tribes. Though there are many interpretations, Kokopelli was usually associated with fertility and abundance.

Tlingit Warrior - Another figure seen painted on the walls of Tiny Town. The Tlingit are an indigenous people of the Pacific Northwest, their influence ranging generally from Alaska down to British Columbia.

Headless Ghosts - After reading this book, you can probably see that there are a lot of legends about headless ghosts. I am not sure why, but this seems to be a common theme found in many legends everywhere. I can only guess that the idea of a headless ghost is scarier than a ghost with a head, and so when people relate these stories to each other they sometimes add a headless ghost just to make the story more frightening. The headless ghost theme may have started with Washington Irving's The Legend of Sleepy Hollow which was itself based on an old German folk story. You may notice that one of my real-life paranormal experiences took place on a local road called Spooky Hollow Road, which is very close to a road named... yes, you guessed it. *Sleepy* Hollow Road.

Headless Brides and Devil Dogs

www.ingramcontent.com/pod-product-compliance
Lightning Source LLC
Chambersburg PA
CBHW031651040426
42453CB00006B/266